Fun Quilt Techniques and Color Concepts

Fresh CUTS

by Debbie Mumm

Dear Friends,

Try something new for a fresh view on quilting and color! This fabulous new book, **FRESH CUTS**, focuses on color, technique, embellishment, and today's unique fabric cuts.

Specialty Cuts features quilts and sewing projects that take advantage of specialty fabric cuts such as jelly rolls, fat quarters, charm packs and layer cakes. In **Fun Techniques**, we'll show you simple ways to create curves, a unique trapunto treatment and easy paper piecing. Explore bold, trendy or vintage fabric combinations in **Colorful Concepts**. And to round out this jam packed book, **Appliqué & Embellishments** provides you with whimsical appliqué designs along with ideas to customize your projects with decorative stiching, buttons & beads.

The choices are abundant and inspiring, so pick your favorites and make your own fresh quilting creations.

Best & Have Fun Always!
Debbie Mumm

©2010 by Debbie Mumm • Leisure Arts, Inc., 5701 Ranch Drive, Little Rock, AR 72223 • www.leisurearts.com

Table of CONTENTS

Specialty cuts

Colorful concepts

Fun techniques

Appliqué & embellishments

Specialty cuts

Specialty Cuts

Fat Quarters, Jelly Rolls, Charm Packs, Oh My! Most of us can't resist the intriguing fabric specialty cuts that are available in fabric shops today. These precut fabrics can present a challenge when planning for quilts, so quilts in this section will give you lots of opportunity to use specialty cut fabrics.

Crisscross Lap Quilt

Intersecting lines weave in and out across this quilt making it appear more complex than it really is. An eye-catching combination of colors and patterns gives this quilt plenty of panache!

Crisscross Lap Quilt Finished Size: 46¼" x 59¾"	FIRST CUT		SECOND CUT	
	Number of Strips or Pieces	Dimensions	Number of Pieces	Dimensions
Fabric A Block Light ⅔ yard	8	2½" x 42"	36 / 36	2½" x 5" / 2½" squares
Fabric B-1 Block Medium Fat Quarter	2 / 4 / 5	5" squares / 2½" x 5" / 2½" squares		
Fabric B-2 Block Medium Fat Quarter	2 / 4 / 4	5" squares / 2½" x 5" / 2½" squares		
Fabric B-3 Block Medium Fat Quarter	2 / 5 / 5	5" squares / 2½" x 5" / 2½" squares		
Fabric B-4 Block Medium Fat Quarter	2 / 5 / 4	5" squares / 2½" x 5" / 2½" squares		
Fabric B-5 Block Medium Fat Quarter	2 / 5 / 5	5" squares / 2½" x 5" / 2½" squares		
Fabric B-6 Block Medium Fat Quarter	2 / 5 / 4	5" squares / 2½" x 5" / 2½" squares		
Fabric B-7 Block Medium Fat Quarter	3 / 4 / 4	5" squares / 2½" x 5" / 2½" squares		
Fabric B-8 Block Medium Fat Quarter	3 / 4 / 5	5" squares / 2½" x 5" / 2½" squares		
Fabric C Lattice Dark ⅝ yard	12	1½" x 42"	48	1½" x 9"
Fabric D Lattice Light Squares & Triangles ⅙ yard	1 / 1	2¾" x 42" / 1½" x 42"	4 / 17	2¾" squares* *cut twice diagonally / 1½" squares
Fabric E Background Triangles ⅞ yard	2	13⅜" x 42"	3 / 2	13⅜" squares* *cut twice diagonally / 7" squares** **cut once diagonally
First Border ¼ yard	5	1" x 42"		
Outside Border ⅝ yard	6	2¾" x 42"		
Binding ½ yard	6	2¼" x 42" ¼" finished binding		
Backing - 3 yards Batting - 54" x 68"				

Fabric Requirements and Cutting Instructions

Read all instructions before beginning and use ¼"-wide seam allowances throughout. Read Cutting Strips and Pieces on page 108 prior to cutting fabric.

Getting Started

This quilt looks complex, but is really a variation of a traditional Nine-Patch Block using different size square and rectangle pieces. This easy-to-make multi-color block measures 9" square (unfinished). Refer to Accurate Seam Allowance on page 108. Whenever possible use Assembly Line Method on page 108. Press seams in direction of arrows.

Making the Blocks

1. Sew one 2½" x 5" Fabric A piece between one 5" Fabric B-5 and one 2½" x 5" Fabric B-1 piece as shown. Press.

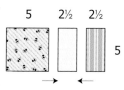

2. Sew one 2½" Fabric B-2 square between one 2½" x 5" Fabric A piece and one 2½" Fabric A square as shown. Press.

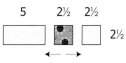

3. Sew one 2½" Fabric A square between one 2½" x 5" Fabric B-3 piece and one 2½" Fabric B-4 square as shown. Press.

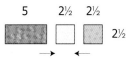

4. Sew unit from step 2 between unit from step 1 and unit from step 3 as shown. Press. Block measures 9" square.

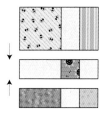

Block measures 9" square

5. Referring to steps 1-4, sew eighteen blocks in assorted Fabric B combinations. Note: Diagram below shows the fabric combinations we used and quantity made for each.

 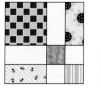

Make 2   Make 3   Make 2

Make 3   Make 2   Make 2

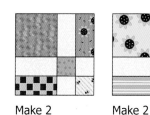

Make 2   Make 2

Assembling the Quilt

These blocks have a definite direction in this quilt. Layout all blocks into rows (setting them on point) prior to sewing. It is important to always check the orientation of these blocks when adding the lattice units in row construction.

1. Sew one 1½" x 9" Fabric C piece between two 1½" Fabric D squares as shown. Press. Make eight and label Unit 1.

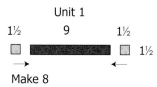

Unit 1

Make 8

2. Sew one 1½" x 9" Fabric C piece between Fabric D triangle pieces as shown. Press. Make two and label Unit 2. Sew one Fabric D triangle piece to one 1½" x 9" Fabric C piece. Press. Make six and label Unit 3. Sew one 1½" x 9" Fabric C piece to one Fabric D triangle piece. Press. Make four and label Unit 4.

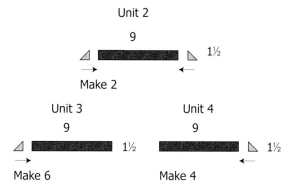

Unit 2

9

Make 2

Unit 3   Unit 4
9   9

Make 6   Make 4

3. Sew one Unit 1 between one Unit 3 and one Unit 4 as shown. Press. Make two.

Make 2

4. Arrange and sew together one Unit 3, two of Unit 1, one 1½" x 9" Fabric C piece, and one Unit 4 as shown. Press. Make two.

Make 2   9   1½

5. Arrange and sew together two of Unit 3, two of Unit 1, two 1½" x 9" Fabric C pieces, and one 1½" Fabric D square as shown. Press.

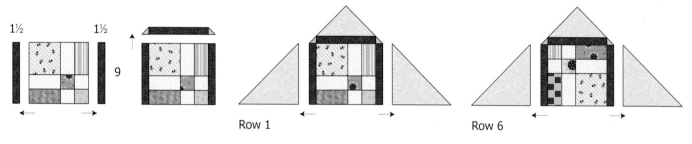

9   9   1½   1½

6. Sew one block between two 1½" x 9" Fabric C pieces as shown. Press. Sew one Unit 2 to this unit. Press. Sew one small Fabric E triangle to top of unit. Press. Sew two large Fabric E triangles to unit as shown. Press. Make two and label Rows 1 and 6.

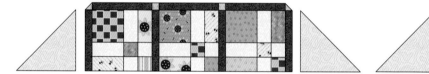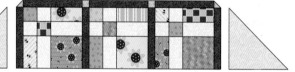

1½   1½   9   Row 1   Row 6

7. Sew four 1½" x 9" Fabric C pieces and three blocks together. Press. Sew unit from step 3 to this unit. Press. Sew two large Fabric E triangles to unit as shown. Press. Make two and label Rows 2 and 5.

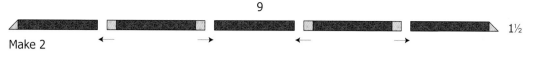

Row 2   Row 5

8. Sew six 1½" x 9" Fabric D pieces and five blocks together. Press. Sew unit from step 4 to this unit. Press. Sew one large Fabric E triangle and one small Fabric E triangle to unit as shown. Press. Make two and label Rows 3 and 4.

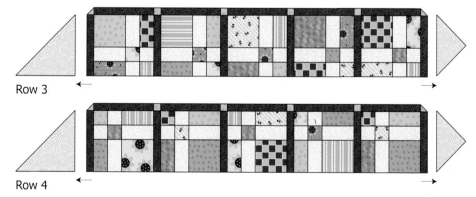

Row 3

Row 4

9. Referring to photo on page 7 and layout on page 10 arrange and sew together rows from steps 6, 7, and 8, and unit from step 5. Press.

Crisscross Lap Quilt
46¼" x 59¾"

Adding the Borders

1. Refer to Adding the Borders on page 110. Measure quilt through center from side to side. Cut two 1"-wide First Border strips to this measurement. Sew to top and bottom of quilt. Press seams toward border.

2. Sew 1" x 42" First Border strips together end-to-end to make one continuous 1"-wide First Border strip. Measure quilt through center from top to bottom including border just added. Cut two 1"-wide First Border strips to this measurement. Sew to sides of quilt. Trim and press.

3. Refer to steps 1 and 2 to join, measure, trim, and sew 2¾" Outside Border strips to top, bottom, and sides of quilt. Press.

Layering and Finishing

1. Cut backing crosswise into two equal pieces. Sew pieces together lengthwise to make one 54" x 80" (approximate) backing piece. Press and trim to 54" x 68".

2. Referring to Layering the Quilt on page 110, arrange and baste backing, batting, and top together. Hand or machine quilt as desired.

3. Refer to Binding the Quilt on page 110. Sew 2¼" x 42" binding strips end-to-end to make one continuous 2¼"-wide binding strip. Bind quilt to finish. Note: Finished width of binding is ¼" instead of our normal ½".

Fresh Chair

Freshen up a chair to complement your pretty quilts. Spray paint and vinyl appliqués transform an old cafeteria chair to a high style accessory.

Painting the Chair

1. Use blue masking tape to mask off areas of the chair that you don't want painted. For this chair, we masked off all the black metal frame and painted only the seat and back.

2. Following manufacturer's directions on spray paint, paint chair in the desired color. Several coats of paint may be needed for good coverage.

3. Select vinyl appliqués to be used. If desired, outline edges of appliqués with permanent marker before removing them from backing. This will provide a hand-painted look to the edges and appliqués will stand out better on a chair that is painted a similar color to appliqués.

4. Apply appliqués following manufacturer's directions.

5. If desired, spray competed chair with a clear sealer for added durability.

Before

SUPPLIES

Old Office or Cafeteria Chair

Spray Paint in Your Choice of Color

Blue Painters Masking Tape

Wallies® Peel and Stick Wall Art Vinyl Appliqués*

Black Permanent Marker (optional)

Clear Spray Sealer

*We used Green Garden #13353 available at www.wallies.com

Center Stripes Lap Quilt

Window centers appear to recede into infinity when striped fabric centers add a modern twist to the traditional Attic Window block. Color placement creates a secondary diagonal design throughout the quilt.

Center Stripes Lap Quilt Finished Size: 41" x 49"	FIRST CUT		SECOND CUT	
	Number of Strips or Pieces	Dimensions	Number of Pieces	Dimensions
Fabric A Stripe Center ½ yard each of 6 Fabrics	2*	6" x 42" *cut for each fabric	10*	6" squares
Fabric B Light Block Border ¼ yard each of 6 Fabrics	2*	2½" x 42" *cut for each fabric	5* 5* 5*	2½" x 8½" 2½" x 4½" 2½" squares
Fabric C Dark Block Border ¼ yard each of 6 Fabrics	2*	2½" x 42" *cut for each fabric	5* 5* 5*	2½" x 8½" 2½" x 4½" 2½" squares
Binding ½ yard	5	2¾" x 42"		
Backing - 1½ yards (Fabric needs to be at least 45"-wide) Batting - 45" x 54"				

Fabric Requirements and Cutting Instructions

Read all instructions before beginning and use ¼"-wide seam allowances throughout. Read Cutting Strips and Pieces on page 108 prior to cutting fabric.

Getting Started

Add a graphic spin to traditional Attic Window blocks by using striped fabrics for the centers. Block measures 8½" square (unfinished). Refer to Accurate Seam Allowance on page 108. Whenever possible use Assembly Line Method on page 108. Press seams in direction of arrows.

Making the Blocks

Select one of each Fabric A, B and C fabrics to make five matching blocks.

1. Cut ten 6" matching Fabric A squares twice diagonally as shown. Only two triangles will be used from each cut square. Note diagram for selected pieces.

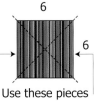

Use these pieces
Cut 10 twice diagonally

TIP

Jelly Rolls and Layer Cake Fabric Packs

This quilt can be made using 2½" strips from a Jelly Roll pack and cutting 6" squares from Layer Cake packs. Using these packs may result in a scrappier quilt since the number of matching blocks that can be made may vary depending on variety of fabrics in the packs.

Center Stripes Lap Quilt
41" x 49"

4. Sew one unit from step 3 between one 2½" x 4½" Fabric B piece and one 2½" x 4½" Fabric C piece as shown. Press. Make five.

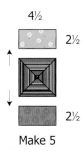

Make 5

5. Refer to Quick Corner Triangles on page 108. Making a quick corner triangle unit, sew one 2½" Fabric C square to one 2½" x 8½" Fabric B piece as shown. Press. Make five.

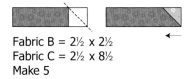

Fabric C = 2½ x 2½
Fabric B = 2½ x 8½
Make 5

6. Making a quick corner triangle unit, sew one 2½" Fabric B square to one 2½" x 8½" Fabric C piece as shown. Press. Make five.

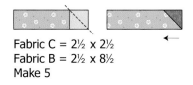

Fabric B = 2½ x 2½
Fabric C = 2½ x 8½
Make 5

7. Sew one unit from step 4 between one unit from step 5 and one unit from step 6 as shown. Press. Make five. Block measures 8½" square. Note: Some seams may need to be re-pressed in the opposite direction when sewing rows together.

Make 5
Block meaures 8½" square

2. Sew two triangles from step 1 together as shown. Press. Make ten.

Make 10

3. Sew two units from step 2 together as shown. Refer to Twisting Seams on page 108 and press. Square unit to 4½". Make five.

Square to 4½
Make 5

8. Repeat steps 1-7 to make a total of twenty-five additional blocks, five of each fabric combination.

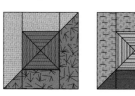

Make 5

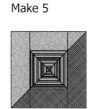

Make 5

Make 5

Make 5

Make 5

Specialty Fabric Cuts

Honey Bun	1½"-wide strips
Jelly Roll	2½"-wide strips
Dessert Roll	5"-wide strips
Charm Pack	5" squares
Layer Cake	10" squares
Brick	5" x 9½" pieces
Fat Quarter	18" x 21"
Obese Eighths	9" x 21"

TIP

Assembling the Quilt

1. Referring to photo on page 13 and layout on page 14, arrange and sew six rows with five blocks each. Press seams in opposite directions from row to row.

2. Sew rows together, repressing seams as needed. Press.

Layering and Finishing

1. Referring to Layering the Quilt on page 110, arrange and baste backing, batting, and top together. Hand or machine quilt as desired.

2. Refer to Binding the Quilt on page 110. Sew 2¾" x 42" binding strips end-to-end to make one continuous 2¾"-wide binding strip. Bind quilt to finish.

Squares on Squares
Table Quilt

Squares making squares and squares on point are encased in sashing on this easy and interesting table quilt. Make it to match your room for a charming table accent.

Squares on Squares Table Quilt Finished Size: 40½" x 40½"	FIRST CUT		SECOND CUT	
	Number of Strips or Pieces	Dimensions	Number of Pieces	Dimensions
Fabric A Background 1¼ yards	3	4½" x 42"	24	4½" squares** **cut once diagonally
	1	2½" x 42"	2	2½" x 21"
	15	1½" x 42"	26	1½" x 7½"
			39	1½" x 5½"
Fabric B Block 1 & Block 2 Center ⅓ yard	2	2½" x 42"		
	1	1½" x 42"	1	1½" x 21"
	1	1" x 42"	16	1" squares
Fabric C Block 1 ¼ yard	2	2½" x 42"		
Fabric D Block 2 Squares ¼ yard each of 2 Fabrics	2*	2½" x 42" *cut for each fabric		
Fabric E Lattice ⅓ yard	8	1" x 42"	40	1" x 7½"
Outside Border ¼ yard	4	1¾" x 42"	2	1¾" x 40½"
			2	1¾" x 37½"
Binding ⅜ yard	4	2¾" x 42"		
Backing - 2½ yards Batting - 45" x 45"				

Fabric Requirements and Cutting Instructions

Read all instructions before beginning and use ¼"-wide seam allowances throughout. Read Cutting Strips and Pieces on page 108 prior to cutting fabric.

Getting Started

These blocks are simple to make and a twist to the setting gives the quilt interest and a little playfulness. Block measures 7½" square (unfinished). Refer to Accurate Seam Allowance on page 108. Whenever possible use Assembly Line Method on page 108. Press seams in direction of arrows.

Making Block 1

1. Sew one 1½" x 42" Fabric A strip between one 2½" x 42" Fabric B strip and one 2½" x 42" Fabric C strip as shown to make a strip set. Press seams toward Fabric A. Cut strip set into twenty-six 2½"-wide segments. Make two.

2½

Make 2
Cut 26 segments

TIP

Jelly Rolls Packs

The blocks in this quilt can be made using light and dark 2½" strips from a Jelly Roll pack. Yardage is needed for the background and lattice fabric. If desired, each block background can be made using a different fabric from Layer Cake fabric packs or assorted Fat Quarters.

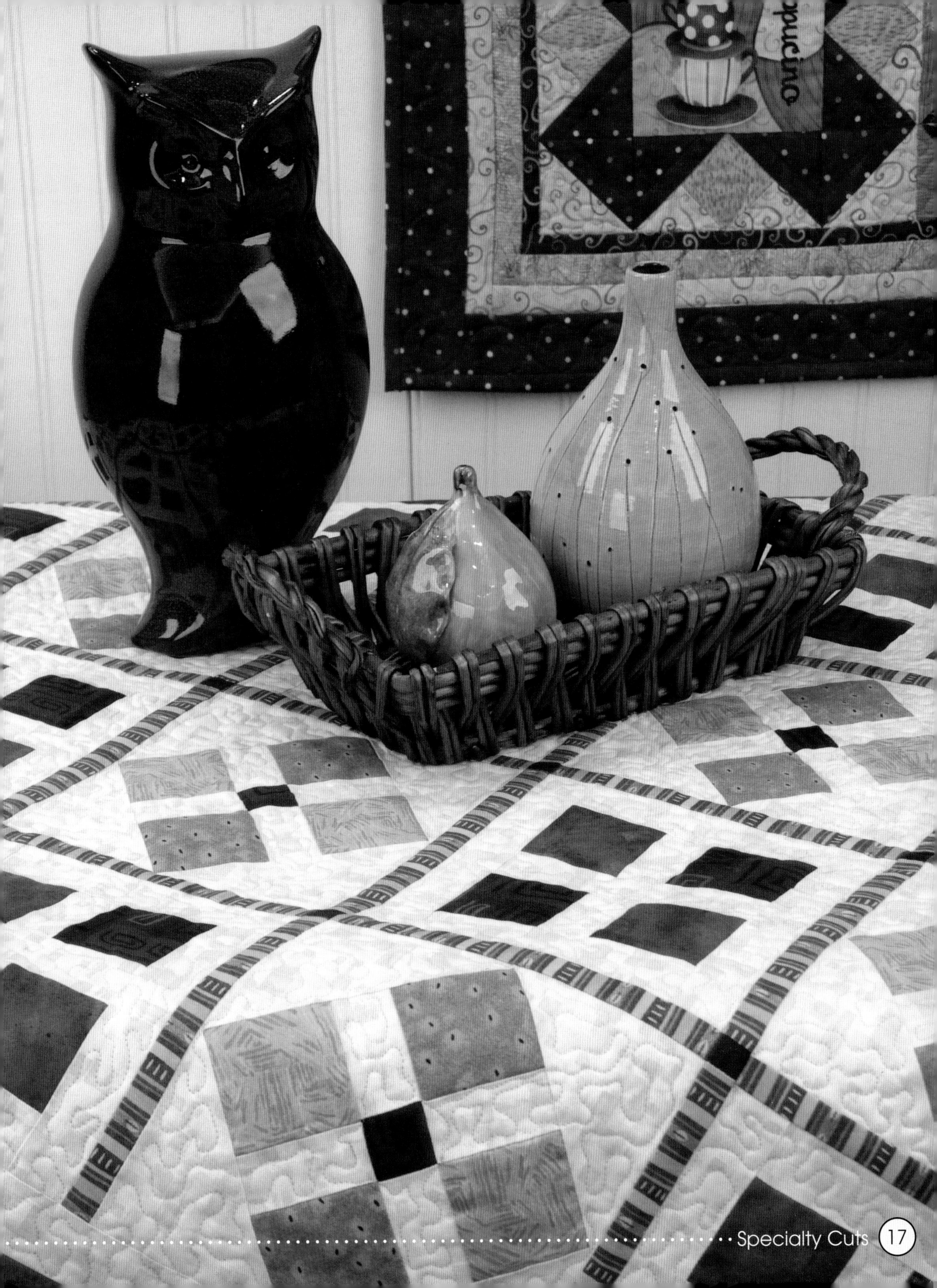

Squares on Squares Table Quilt
40½" x 40½"

2. Sew one 1½" x 5½" Fabric A strip between two units from step 1 as shown. Press. Make thirteen.

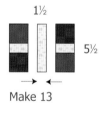

1½

5½

Make 13

3. Sew one unit from step 2 between two 1½" x 5½" Fabric A pieces. Press seams toward Fabric A. Sew this unit between two 1½" x 7½" Fabric A pieces as shown. Press. Make thirteen and label Block 1. Block 1 measures 7½" square.

Block 1

1½   1½

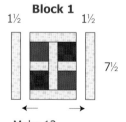

7½

Make 13
Block measures 7½" square

Making Block 2

1. Sew one 1½" x 42" Fabric A strip between two different 2½" x 42" Fabric D strips as shown to make a strip set. Press seams toward Fabric A. Make two. Cut strip set into twenty-four 2½"-wide segments.

2½

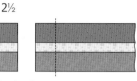

Make 2
Cut 24 segments

2. Sew one 1½" x 21" Fabric B strip between two 2½" x 21" Fabric A strips as shown to make a strip set. Press seams toward Fabric A. Cut strip set into twelve 1½"-wide segments.

1½

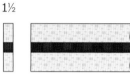

Cut 12 segments

3. Sew one unit from step 2 between two units from step 1 as shown. Press. Make twelve.

Make 12

4. Sew four Fabric A triangles to one unit from step 3 as shown. Press seams toward triangles. Note: Triangle ends extend past unit edge as shown. Make twelve and label Block 2. Block 2 measures 7½" square.

Block 2

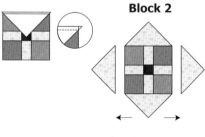

Make 12
Block measures 7½" square

Assembling the Quilt

Layout all blocks into rows prior to sewing the quilt top. Refer to photo on page 17 and layout on page 18 for all assembling steps.

1. Arrange and sew together three of Block 1, two of Block 2, and four 1" x 7½" Fabric E pieces. Press. Make three.

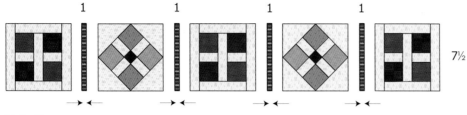

Make 3

2. Arrange and sew together three of Block 2, two of Block 1, and four 1" x 7½" Fabric E pieces. Press. Make two.

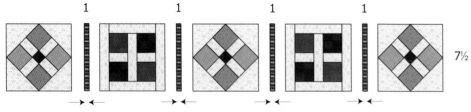

Make 2

3. Arrange and sew together five 1" x 7½" Fabric E pieces and four 1" Fabric B squares. Press. Make four.

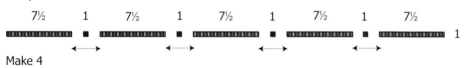

Make 4

4. Arrange and sew rows from steps 1-3 together to make quilt top. Press.

5. Sew two 1¾" x 37½" Outside Border strips to top and bottom of quilt. Press seams toward border.

6. Sew two 1¾" x 40" Outside Border strips to sides of quilt. Press.

Layering and Finishing

1. Cut backing crosswise into two equal pieces. Sew pieces together lengthwise to make one 45" x 80" (approximate) backing piece. Press and trim to 45" x 45".

2. Referring to Layering the Quilt on page 110, arrange and baste backing, batting, and top together. Hand or machine quilt as desired.

3. Refer to Binding the Quilt on page 110. Use 2¾"-wide binding strips to bind quilt.

Fandago
Lap Quilt

The creative placement of light, medium, and dark fabrics puts the emphasis on different elements in this cozy, country-style, lap quilt. Blocks are based on the traditional Jack-in-the-Box pattern.

Fandango Lap Quilt Finished Size: 51" x 61"	FIRST CUT		SECOND CUT	
	Number of Strips or Pieces	Dimensions	Number of Pieces	Dimensions
Fabric A Block Background ½ yard each of 8 Fabrics	4*	3" x 42" *cut for each fabric	48*	3" squares
Fabric B Large Triangle Accent ⅓ yard each of 8 Fabrics	3*	3" x 42" *cut for each fabric	16*	3" x 5½"
Fabric C Diamond Accent ⅓ yard each of 8 Fabrics	3*	3" x 42" *cut for each fabric	16*	3" x 5½"
Fabric D Center ¼ yard each of 8 Fabrics	2*	3" x 42" *cut for each fabric	16*	3" squares
Binding ⅝ yard	6	2¾" x 42"		

Backing - 3¼ yards
Batting - 57" x 67"

Fabric Requirements and Cutting Instructions

Read all instructions before beginning and use ¼"-wide seam allowances throughout. Read Cutting Strips and Pieces on page 108 prior to cutting fabric.

Getting Started

Each block in this quilt has a different look depending on color placement. Block measures 10½" square (unfinished). Refer to Accurate Seam Allowance on page 108. Whenever possible use Assembly Line Method on page 108. Press seams in direction of arrows.

TIP

Fat Quarter Fabrics

Fat Quarter fabric (18" x 21") can be used for Fabrics B, C, and D pieces. If you prefer, use sixteen assorted Fat Quarter pieces for Fabric A and cut twenty-four 3" squares from each. This will make thirty-two blocks, two blocks for each Fabric A piece.

Fandango Lap Quilt
51" x 61"

2. Making quick corner triangles, sew one 3" Fabric A square and one 3" Fabric D square to one 3" x 5½" Fabric C piece as shown. Press. Make sixteen.

Fabric A = 3 x 3
Fabric D = 3 x 3
Fabric C = 3 x 5½
Make 16

3. Sew one unit from step 1 to one unit from step 2 as shown. Press. Make sixteen.

Make 16

Making the Blocks

1. Refer to Quick Corner Triangles on page 108. Making quick corner triangle units, sew two 3" Fabric A squares to one 3" x 5½" Fabric B piece as shown. Press. Make sixteen.

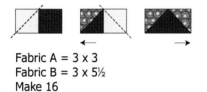

Fabric A = 3 x 3
Fabric B = 3 x 5½
Make 16

4. Sew two units from step 3 together as shown. Press. Make eight. Sew two of these units together. Refer to Twisting Seams on page 108 and press. Make four. Block measures 10½" square.

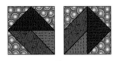
Make 8

Make 4
Block measures 10½" square

5. Referring to steps 1-4, make twenty-eight additional blocks, four of each combination as shown.

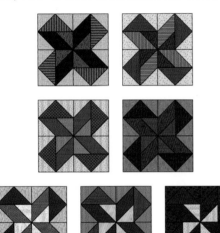

Make 28
(four of each combination)

Assembling the Quilt

Layout the entire quilt prior to sewing rows together. Two extra blocks were made to give block placement options when laying out the quilt.

1. Referring to photo on page 21 and layout on page 22, arrange and sew together six rows with five blocks each. Press seams in the opposite direction from row to row.

2. Sew rows together. Press.

Layering and Finishing

1. Cut backing crosswise into two equal pieces. Sew pieces together lengthwise to make one 58" x 80" (approximate) backing piece. Press and trim to 58" x 67".

2. Referring to Layering the Quilt on page 110, arrange and baste backing, batting, and top together. Hand or machine quilt as desired.

3. Refer to Binding the Quilt on page 110. Sew 2¾" x 42" binding strips end-to-end to make one continuous 2¾"-wide binding strip. Bind quilt to finish.

Main Focus
Wall Quilt

Make a favorite motif the center of attention using this X-traordinary pattern! We chose a coffee motif, but any themed fabric in the right size can be used to create a decorative wall quilt.

Main Focus Wall Quilt Finished Size: 38½" x 38½"	FIRST CUT		SECOND CUT	
	Number of Strips or Pieces	Dimensions	Number of Pieces	Dimensions
Fabric A Block 1 Background ½ yard	1 4	3½" x 42" 3" x 42"	10 40	3½" squares 3" squares
Fabric B Block 1 Dark Accent ½ yard	1 4	3½" x 42" 3" x 42"	10 40	3½" squares 3" squares
Fabric C Block 1 Small Squares ⅓ yard	3	3" x 42"	20	3" x 5½"
Fabric D Block 1 & 2 Centers ½ yard	9	5½" squares* *Fussy Cut Yardage may vary depending on fabric selected.		
Fabric E Block 2 Background ½ yard	1 3	3½" x 42" 3" x 42"	8 32	3½" squares 3" squares
Fabric F Block 2 Dark Accent ½ yard	1 3	3½" x 42" 3" x 42"	8 32	3½" squares 3" squares
Fabric G Block 2 Small Squares ⅓ yard	3	3" x 42"	16	3" x 5½"
First Border ⅙ yard	4	1" x 42"	2 2	1" x 31½" 1" x 30½"
Second Border ¼ yard	4	1¼" x 42"	2 2	1¼" x 33" 1¼" x 31½"
Third Border ¼ yard	4	1¼" x 42"	2 2	1¼" x 34½" 1¼" x 33"
Outside Border ⅓ yard	4	2¼" x 42"	2 2	2¼" x 38" 2¼" x 34½"
Binding ⅜ yard	4	2¾" x 42"		

Backing - 1¼ yards (Fabric needs to be at least 45"-wide)
Batting - 43" x 43"

Fabric Requirements and Cutting Instructions

Read all instructions before beginning and use ¼"-wide seam allowances throughout. Read Cutting Strips and Pieces on page 108 prior to cutting fabric.

Getting Started

You can almost smell the coffee brewing while feasting your eyes on this scrumptious wall quilt. Block measures 10½" square (unfinished). Refer to Accurate Seam Allowance on page 108. Whenever possible use Assembly Line Method on page 108. Press seams in direction of arrows.

Making Block 1

1. Refer to Quick Corner Triangles on page 108. Making quick corner triangle units, sew two 3" Fabric A squares to one 3" x 5½" Fabric C piece as shown. Press. Make twenty.

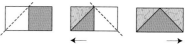

Fabric A = 3 x 3
Fabric C = 3 x 5½
Make 20

2. Making quick corner triangle units, sew two 3" Fabric B squares to one unit from step 1 as shown. Press. Make twenty.

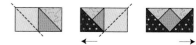

Fabric B = 3 x 3
Unit from step 1
Make 20

Main Focus Wall Quilt
38½" x 38½"

5. Sew one unit from step 2 between two units from step 3 as shown. Press. Make ten.

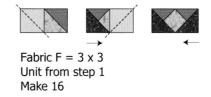

Make 10

6. Sew one unit from step 4 between two units from step 5 as shown. Press. Make five and label Block 1. Block measures 10½" square.

Block 1

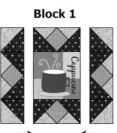

Make 5
Block measures 10½" square

Making Block 2

1. Refer to Quick Corner Triangles on page 108. Making quick corner triangle units, sew two 3" Fabric E squares to one 3" x 5½" Fabric G piece as shown. Press. Make sixteen.

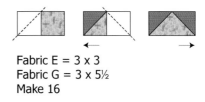

Fabric E = 3 x 3
Fabric G = 3 x 5½
Make 16

2. Making quick corner triangle units, sew two 3" Fabric F squares to one unit from step 1 as shown. Press. Make sixteen.

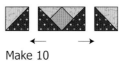

Fabric F = 3 x 3
Unit from step 1
Make 16

3. Draw a diagonal line on wrong side of one 3½" Fabric A square. Place marked square and one 3½" Fabric B square right sides together. Sew scant ¼" away from drawn line on both sides to make half-square triangles as shown. Make ten. Cut on drawn line and press. Square to 3". This will make twenty half-square triangle units.

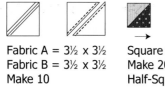

Fabric A = 3½ x 3½   Square to 3"
Fabric B = 3½ x 3½   Make 20
Make 10   Half-Square Triangle Units

4. Sew one 5½" Fabric D square between two units from step 2 as shown. Press. Make five.

5½

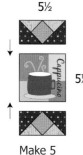

5½

Make 5

3. Draw a diagonal line on wrong side of one 3½" Fabric E square. Place marked square and one 3½" Fabric F square right sides together. Sew scant ¼" away from drawn line on both sides to make half-square triangles as shown. Make eight. Cut on drawn line and press. Square to 3". This will make sixteen half-square triangle units.

Fabric E = 3½ x 3½   Square to 3"
Fabric F = 3½ x 3½   Make 16
Make 8   Half-Square Triangle Units

4. Sew one 5½" Fabric D square between two units from step 2 as shown. Press. Make four.

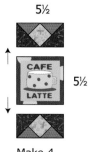

5½

5½

Make 4

5. Sew one unit from step 2 between two units from step 3 as shown. Press. Make eight.

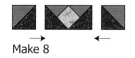

Make 8

6. Sew one unit from step 4 between two units from step 5 as shown. Press. Make four and label Block 2. Block measures 10½" square.

Block 2

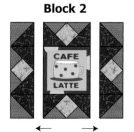

Make 4
Block measures 10½" square

Assembling the Quilt

1. Referring to photo on page 25 and layout on page 26, sew one Block 2 between two of Block 1. Press seams toward Block 1. Make two.

2. Referring to photo on page 25 and layout on page 26, sew one Block 1 between two of Block 2. Press seams toward Block 1.

3. Referring to photo on page 25 and layout on page 26, sew row from step 2 between rows from step 1. Press.

4. Sew quilt top between two 1" x 30½" First Border strips. Press seams toward border. Sew this unit between two 1" x 31½" First Border strips. Press.

5. Sew quilt top between two 1¼" x 31½" Second Border strips. Press seams toward border just added. Sew this unit between two 1¼" x 33" Second Border strips. Press.

6. Sew quilt top between two 1¼" x 33" Third Border strips. Press seams toward border just added. Sew this unit between two 1¼" x 34½" Third Border strips. Press.

7. Sew quilt top between two 2¼" x 34½" Outside Border strips. Press seams toward border just added. Sew this unit between two 2¼" x 38" Outside Border strips. Press.

Layering and Finishing

1. Referring to Layering the Quilt on page 110, arrange and baste backing, batting, and top together. Hand or machine quilt as desired.

2. Refer to Binding the Quilt on page 110. Sew 2¾" x 42" binding strips end-to-end to make one continuous 2¾"-wide binding strip. Bind quilt to finish.

Favorite Fabric
Table Runner

Love a particular fabric? Make a fast and fabulous table runner to show it off. Choose from two variations to make the perfect runner for your table.

Favorite Fabric Table Runner Finished Size: 13" x 30" each	FIRST CUT	
	Number of Strips or Pieces	Dimensions
Coffee Table Runner		
Fabric A Main Fabric ½ yard	1 2	9½" x 22½" 1½" x 29½"
Fabric B Motif Accent ¼ yard	2	4" x 9½"* *Fussy Cut
Fabric C Accent Border & Binding ⅜ yard	3 2	2¾" x 42" 1" x 29½"
Simple Table Runner		
Fabric A Main Fabric ½ yard	1 2	9½" x 29½" 1½" x 29½"
Fabric C Accent Border & Binding ⅜ yard	3 2	2¾" x 42" 1" x 29½"
Backing - 1 yard (Makes 2 Backing Pieces) **Batting - 17" x 34"** (for each)		

Fabric Requirements and Cutting Instructions

Read all instructions before beginning and use ¼"-wide seam allowances throughout. Read Cutting Strips and Pieces on page 108 prior to cutting fabric.

Getting Started

These quick-to-make table runners are a great way to showcase a favorite fabric. Refer to Accurate Seam Allowance on page 108. Press seams in direction of arrows.

Making the Coffee Table Runner

1. Sew 9½" x 22½" Fabric A piece between two 4" x 9½" Fabric B pieces as shown. Press.

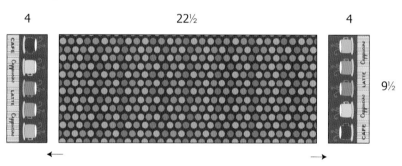

2. Arrange and sew together two 1½" x 29½" Fabric A pieces, two 1" x 29½" Fabric C strips and unit from step 1. Press.

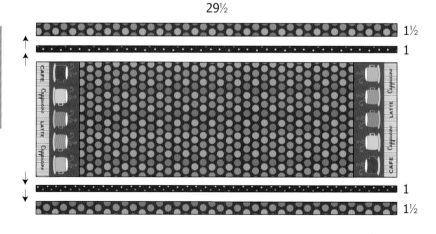

Coffee Table Runner

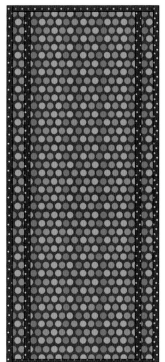

Simple Table Runner

Making the Simple Table Runner

Referring to Simple Table Runner layout, arrange and sew together two 1½" x 29½" Fabric A pieces, two 1" x 29½" Fabric C strips and 9½" x 29½" Fabric A piece. Press.

Layering and Finishing

1. Referring to Layering the Quilt on page 110, arrange and baste backing, batting, and top together. Hand or machine quilt as desired.

2. Refer to Binding the Quilt on page 110. Use 2¾"-wide Binding strips to bind quilt.

Colorful
concepts

FABRIC Swatches

Debbie Mumm
QUILT CLASSIC

- 67251-200 Espresso
- 67252-222 Mocha Brown
- 67251-330 Garnet
- 67251-440 Blue Glacier
- 67252-500 Ochre
- 67251-700 Dark Fern
- 67252-505 Dark Ochre
- 67251-770 Light Basil
- 67251-800 Spice Orange
- 67252-808 Dark Spice
- 67251-722 Eternally Tan
- 67252-444 Deep Blue Sea

Colorful Concepts

Color is both a quilter's greatest challenge and her greatest opportunity. Regardless of the block design selected, color determines whether the quilt will be contemporary, vintage, traditional, or whimsical. Projects in this chapter explore several intriguing color concepts, but review all the quilts in this book when selecting a fresh new color scheme for your next quilt.

Chinese Coins Wall Art

Chinese Coins units go modern with bold contemporary colors organized in a pattern that gives a feeling of movement and dimension to these stunning banners. Strong lines are offset by circular quilting contributing to the illusion of flowing motion.

Chinese Coins Wall Art Finished Size: 15" x 42½" each	FIRST CUT		SECOND CUT	
	Number of Strips or Pieces	Dimensions	Number of Pieces	Dimensions
Fabric A #1 Light ⅛ yard each of 3 Fabrics	1*	2" x 42" *cut for each fabric		
Fabric B #2 Light Medium ⅙ yard each of 3 Fabrics	2*	2" x 42" *cut for each fabric		
Fabric C #3 Medium ⅙ yard each of 3 Fabrics	2*	2" x 42" *cut for each fabric		
Fabric D #4 Medium Dark ⅙ yard each of 3 Fabrics	2*	2" x 42" *cut for each fabric		
Fabric E #5 Dark ⅙ yard each of 3 Fabrics	2*	2" x 42" *cut for each fabric		
Fabric F Sashing ⅜ yard	11	1" x 42"	5 4	1" x 41" 1" x 13½"
Binding ⅝ yard	6	2¾" x 42"		
Backing - 1⅓ yards (Makes 2 Backing Pieces) Batting - 19" x 47" (for each)				

Fabric Requirements and Cutting Instructions

Read all instructions before beginning and use ¼"-wide seam allowances throughout. Read Cutting Strips and Pieces on page 108 prior to cutting fabric.

Getting Started

These stunning banners shimmer with light and dark shades of fabric creating a sense of light and motion. Refer to Accurate Seam Allowance on page 108. Whenever possible use Assembly Line Method on page 108.

Making the Strip Sets

This quilt uses three different colorways (orange, yellow, and green) but can be made using any color combination to fit your decorating style. The instructions given reflect our color combination.

TIP

Colorful Concept

To make the quilt shimmer, use gradating shades of light to dark fabrics in the same color family. Layout selected fabrics so only a small section of each shows. Check color transition from light to dark. Sometimes when a fabric is placed next to another, the color value changes and will need to be moved or eliminated.

Quilt 1   ## Quilt 2

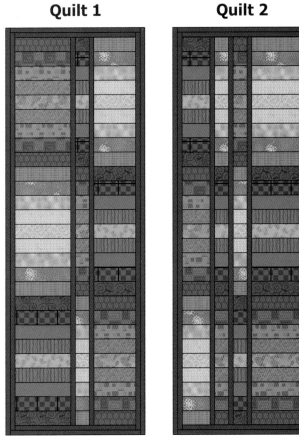

Chinese Coins Wall Art
15" x 42½" each

2. Sew together one 2" x 42" Fabric B strip, one 2" x 42" Fabric C strip, one 2" x 42" Fabric D strip, and one 2" x 42" Fabric E strip as shown. Press seams in one direction.

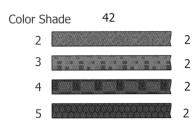

Color Shade	42	
2		2
3		2
4		2
5		2

3. Sew unit from step 1 to unit from step 2 as shown. Press.

4. Repeat steps 1 and 2 to make a total of three strip sets in three different color combinations.

1. Sew together one 2" x 42" Fabric E strip, one 2" x 42" Fabric D strip, one 2" x 42" Fabric C strip, one 2" x 42" Fabric B strip, and one 2" x 42" Fabric A strip as shown to make a strip set. Press seams in one direction.

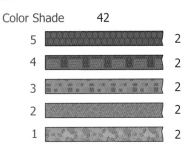

Color Shade	42	
5		2
4		2
3		2
2		2
1		2

5. Cut each strip set into one 6½"-wide segment, one 6"-wide segment, one 5"-wide segment, one 3½"-wide segment, and three 2"-wide segments as shown.

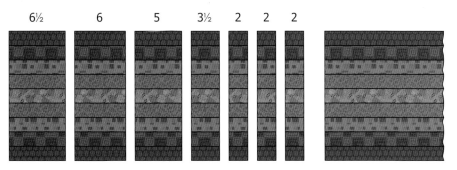

6½   6   5   3½   2   2   2

Cut for each color combination

Assembling the Quilt

Refer to photo on page 33 and layout on page 34 for all assembling steps for unit placement. Press all seams in one direction.

Quilt 1

1. Sew 6½"-wide yellow segment between 6½"-wide orange segment and 6½"-wide green segment. Press.

2. Sew 2"-wide orange segment between 2"-wide green segment and 2"-wide yellow segment. Press.

3. Sew 5"-wide green segment between 5"-wide yellow segment and 5"-wide orange segment. Press.

4. Arrange and sew together unit from step 1, one 1" x 41" Fabric F strip, unit from step 2, one 1" x 41" Fabric F strip, and unit from step 3. Press.

5. Sew two 1" x 13½" Fabric F strips to top and bottom of quilt. Press. Sew 1" x 42" Fabric F strips to sides. Press.

Quilt 2

1. Sew 3½"-wide orange segment between 3½"-wide green segment and 3½"-wide yellow segment. Press.

2. Sew 2"-wide green segment between 2"-wide yellow segment and 2"-wide orange segment. Press.

3. Sew 2"-wide yellow segment between 2"-wide orange segment and 2"-wide green segment. Press.

4. Sew 6"-wide green segment between 6"-wide yellow segment and 6"-wide orange segment. Press.

5. Arrange and sew together unit from step 1, one 1" x 41" Fabric F strip, unit from step 2, one 1" x 41" Fabric F strip, unit from step 3, one 1" x 41" Fabric F strip, and unit from step 4. Press.

6. Sew two 1" x 13½" Fabric F strips to top and bottom of quilt. Press. Sew 1" x 42" Fabric F strips to sides. Press.

Layering and Finishing

1. Referring to Layering the Quilt on page 110, arrange and baste backing, batting, and top together. Hand or machine quilt as desired.

2. Refer to Binding the Quilt on page 110. Use 2¾"-wide Binding strips to bind quilt.

Vintage Lap Quilt

Soft pastel flowers dance on an ivory field on this lap quilt that has a vintage vibe. All the floral fabrics have a muted depth of color which creates a feeling of age and a sense of order in the quilt.

Vintage Lap Quilt Finished Size: 56" x 68"	FIRST CUT		SECOND CUT	
	Number of Strips or Pieces	Dimensions	Number of Pieces	Dimensions
Fabric A Background 3¼ yards	31	3½" x 42"	336	3½" squares
Fabric B Block Pastels ¼ yard each of 7 Fabrics  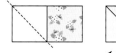	2*	3½" x 42" *cut for each fabric	12*	3½" x 6½"
Fabric C Block Greens ¾ yard each of 2 Fabrics 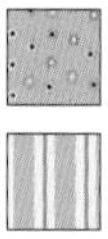	7*	3½" x 42" *cut for each fabric	42*	3½" x 6½"
First Border ¼ yard	6	1" x 42"		
Outside Border ⅔ yard	6	3½" x 42"		
Binding ⅝ yard	7	2¾" x 42"		
Backing - 3½ yards Batting - 62" x 74"				

Fabric Requirements and Cutting Instructions

Read all instructions before beginning and use ¼"-wide seam allowances throughout. Read Cutting Strips and Pieces on page 108 prior to cutting fabric.

Getting Started

Soft pastel fabrics are featured in this tranquil quilt. Block measures 12½" square (unfinished). Refer to Accurate Seam Allowance on page 108. Whenever possible use Assembly Line Method on page 108. Press seams in direction of arrows.

Making the Quilt

Twenty-one blocks will be made, three of each matching combination of fabrics. Note: Only twenty will be used in this quilt.

1. Refer to Quick Corner Triangles on page 108. Making quick corner triangle units, sew two 3½" Fabric A squares to one 3½" x 6½" Fabric B piece as shown. Press. Make eighty-four, twelve of each combination.

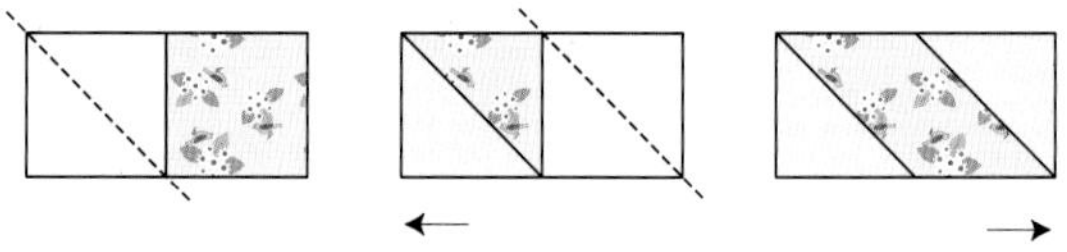

Fabric A = 3½ x 3½
Fabric B = 3½ x 6½
Make 84
(12 of each combination)

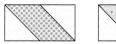

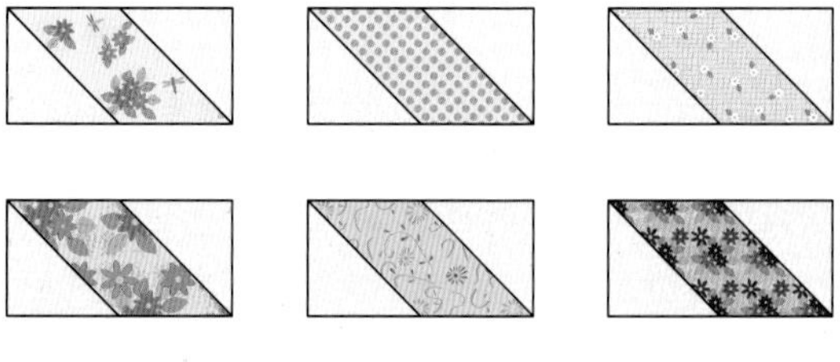

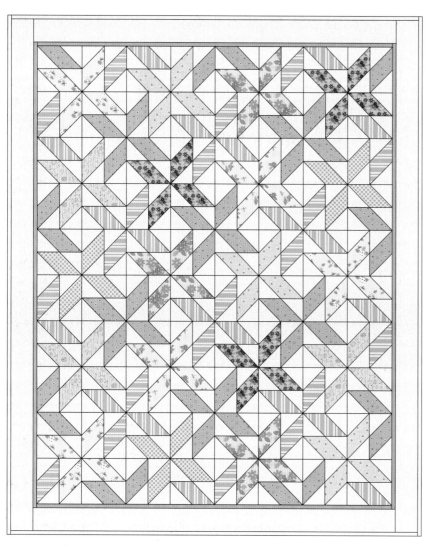

Vintage Lap Quilt
56" x 68"

3. Sew one Unit 1 from step 2 to one unit from step 1 as shown. Press. Make forty-two, six of each combination.

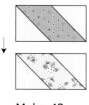

Make 42
(6 of each combination)

4. Sew one Unit 2 from step 2 to one unit from step 1 as shown. Press. Make forty-two, six of each combination.

Make 42
(6 of each combination)

5. Sew one unit from step 3 to one unit from step 4 matching Fabric B pieces. Make forty-two, six of each combination.

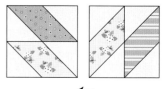

Make 42
(6 of each combination)

6. Sew two units from step 5 together as shown, matching Fabric B pieces. Refer to Twisting Seams on page 108 and press. Make twenty-one, three of each combination. Block measures 12½" square.

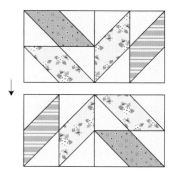

Make 21
(3 of each combination)
Block measures 12½" square

2. Making quick corner triangle units, sew two 3½" Fabric A squares to one 3½" x 6½" Fabric C piece as shown. Press. Make eighty-four, forty-two of each combination. Label one set Unit 1 and the other Unit 2 as shown.

Unit 1

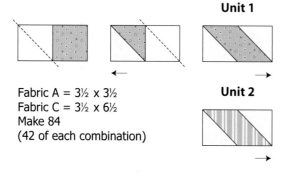

Fabric A = 3½ x 3½
Fabric C = 3½ x 6½
Make 84
(42 of each combination)

Unit 2

Assembling the Quilt

Since this quilt has a scrappy look, layout all blocks into rows prior to sewing the quilt top. Refer to photo on page 37 and layout on page 38.

1. Arrange and sew together five rows with four blocks each. Press seams in opposite direction from row to row.

2. Sew rows together and press.

Adding the Borders

1. Refer to Adding the Borders on page 110. Sew 1" x 42" First Border strips together end-to-end to make one continuous 1"-wide First Border strip. Measure quilt through center from side to side. Cut two 1"-wide First Border strips to this measurement. Sew to top and bottom of quilt. Press seams toward border.

2. Measure quilt through center from top to bottom including borders just added. Cut two 1"-wide First Border strips to this measurement. Sew to sides of quilt. Press.

3. Refer to steps 1 and 2 to join, measure, trim, and sew 3½"-wide Outside Border strips to top, bottom, and sides of quilt. Press.

Layering and Finishing

1. Cut backing crosswise into two equal pieces. Sew pieces together lengthwise to make one 62" x 80" (approximate) backing piece. Press.

2. Referring to Layering the Quilt on page 110, arrange and baste backing, batting, and top together. Hand or machine quilt as desired.

3. Refer to Binding the Quilt on page 110. Sew 2¾" x 42" binding strips end-to-end to make one continuous 2¾"-wide binding strip. Bind quilt to finish.

Pillow Talk

Complete your pastel paradise with a serene pillow that repeats the soothing color scheme.

Making the Pillow

1. Refer to Pastel Quilt step 1 on page 36 to make four units. Press. Referring to photo, sew one 3½" x 6½" Fabric B piece to top of one unit. Press seams toward Fabric B. Make four.

2. Sew two units from step 1 together. Press. Make two. Sew these units together. Press.

3. Sew unit between two 1½" x 12½" First Border strips. Press. Sew this unit between two 1½" x 14½" First Border strips. Press.

4. Sew unit between two 2½" x 14½" Outside Border strips. Press. Sew this unit between two 2½" x 18½" Outside Border strips. Press.

5. Refer to Finishing Pillows on page 111, step 1, to prepare pillow top for quilting. Quilt as desired.

6. Use two 12" x 18½" backing pieces and refer to Finishing Pillows, page 111, steps 2-4, to sew backing. Insert pillow.

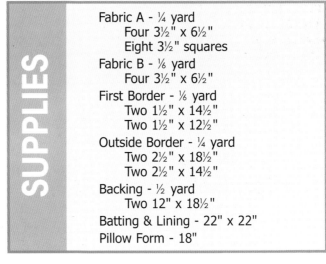

SUPPLIES

Fabric A - ¼ yard
   Four 3½" x 6½"
   Eight 3½" squares
Fabric B - ⅛ yard
   Four 3½" x 6½"
First Border - ⅛ yard
   Two 1½" x 14½"
   Two 1½" x 12½"
Outside Border - ¼ yard
   Two 2½" x 18½"
   Two 2½" x 14½"
Backing - ½ yard
   Two 12" x 18½"
Batting & Lining - 22" x 22"
Pillow Form - 18"

Bravura Lap Quilt

Black, white, and one color is a hot trend among style-savvy quilters and this quilt is a brilliant way to use a vast array of black and white prints with a dollop of your favorite color. Half-Square Triangles make it quick and easy sewing.

Bravura Lap Quilt Finished Size: 43½" x 55½"	FIRST CUT		SECOND CUT	
	Number of Strips or Pieces	Dimensions	Number of Pieces	Dimensions
Fabric A Lights ¼ yard each of 8 Fabrics	1*	5" x 42" *cut for each fabric	8*	5" squares
Fabric B Darks ¼ yard each of 8 Fabrics	1* 1*	5" x 42" 1¾" x 42" *cut for each fabric	8* 4* 4*	5" squares 1¾" x 4½" 1¾" x 2"
Fabric C Green Accent ⅓ yard	5	1¾" x 42"	22 22	1¾" x 4½" 1¾" x 2"
Fabric D Center ⅙ yard	2	2" x 42"	27	2" squares
First Border ¼ yard	5	1" x 42"	2	1" x 36½"
Second Border ¼ yard	5	1¼" x 42"	2	1¼" x 37½"
Outside Border ½ yard	5	2½" x 42"	2	2½" x 39"
Binding ⅝ yard	6	2¾" x 42"		
Backing - 2¾ yards Batting - 49" x 61"				

Fabric Requirements and Cutting Instructions

Read all instructions before beginning and use ¼"-wide seam allowances throughout. Read Cutting Strips and Pieces on page 108 prior to cutting fabric.

Getting Started

Sparks of green accent this scrappy black and white quilt. Refer to Accurate Seam Allowance on page 108. Whenever possible use Assembly Line Method on page 108. Press seams in direction of arrows.

Making the Quilt

1. Sew one 2" Fabric D square between two 1¾" x 2" Fabric B pieces. Sew this unit between two matching 1¾" x 4½" Fabric B pieces as shown. Press and label Unit 1. Make sixteen in assorted Fabric B combinations.

Unit 1

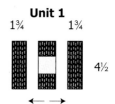

Make 16 (in assorted Fabric B combinations)

TIP

Colorful Concept

Have fun using assorted black and white fabrics to create this quilt. Use yardage listed in chart or black and white Dessert Rolls (5" x 42") or Charm Packs (5" squares).

2. Sew one 2" Fabric D square between two 1¾" x 2" Fabric C pieces. Sew this unit between two 1¾" x 4½" Fabric C pieces as shown. Press and label Unit 2. Make eleven.

Unit 2

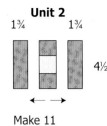

Make 11

3. Draw a diagonal line on wrong side of one 5" Fabric A square. Place marked square and one 5" Fabric B square right sides together. Sew scant ¼" away from drawn line on both sides to make half-square triangles as shown. Make sixty-four. Cut on drawn line and press. Square to 4½". Label these Unit 3. This will make one hundred twenty-eight half-square triangle units. Only eighty-six units will be used in this quilt; extras were made to allow for fabric placement options.

Unit 3

Fabric A = 5 x 5
Fabric B = 5 x 5
Make 64

Square to 4½"
Make 128
Half-Square Triangle units

Note: Only 86 Half-Square Triangle units will be used in quilt; extras are made for fabric placement options and can be used for Bravura Tote (page 45).

Assembling the Quilt

Refer to photo on page 41, layout on page 44, and step diagrams. Layout the entire quilt top prior to sewing. Select the half-square triangle units for the quilt and save extra ones for a future project. Note: Bravura Tote project (page 45) uses forty of the unused units.

1. Arrange and sew together one Unit 1, seven of Unit 3, and one Unit 2 as shown. Press. Make two and label Rows 1 & 6. Press row 6 in the opposite direction.

Make 2
Press Row 6 in the opposite direction
Label Rows 1 & 6

2. Arrange and sew together seven of Unit 3, one Unit 2, and one Unit 1 as shown. Press. Make three and label Rows 2, 7, and 12. Press row 7 in the opposite direction.

Make 3
Press Row 7 in the opposite direction
Label Rows 2, 7 & 12

3. Arrange and sew together eight of Unit 3 and one Unit 1 as shown. Press. Make two and label Rows 3 & 8. Press row 8 in the opposite direction.

Make 2
Press Row 8 in the opposite direction
Label Rows 3 & 8

4. Arrange and sew together seven of Unit 3, one Unit 1, and one Unit 2 as shown. Press. Make two and label Rows 4 & 9. Press row 9 in the opposite direction.

Make 2
Press Row 9 in the opposite direction
Label Rows 4 & 9

5. Arrange and sew together seven of Unit 3, one Unit 2, and one Unit 1 as shown. Press and label Row 5.

Label Row 5

6. Arrange and sew together seven of Unit 3 and two of Unit 2 as shown. Press and label Row 10.

Label Row 10

7. Arrange and sew together one Unit 2, seven of Unit 3, and one of Unit 1 as shown. Press and label Row 11.

Label Row 11

8. Referring to photo on page 41 and layout on page 44, arrange and sew together rows from steps 1-7. Press.

3. Refer to steps 1 and 2 to join, measure, trim, and sew 1¼"-wide Second Border strips, and 2½"-wide Outside Border strips to top, bottom, and sides of quilt. Press. Note: Top and bottom border strips for Second and Outside Borders are listed in chart.

Layering and Finishing

1. Cut backing crosswise into two equal pieces. Sew pieces together lengthwise to make one 49" x 80" (approximate) backing piece. Press and trim to 49" x 61".

2. Referring to Layering the Quilt on page 110, arrange and baste backing, batting, and top together. Hand or machine quilt as desired.

3. Refer to Binding the Quilt on page 110. Sew 2¾" x 42" binding strips end-to-end to make one continuous 2¾"-wide binding strip. Bind quilt to finish.

Bravura Lap Quilt
43½" x 55½"

Adding the Borders

1. Refer to Adding the Borders on page 110. Sew two 1" x 36½" First Border strips to top and bottom of quilt. Press seams toward border.

2. Measure quilt through center from top to bottom including borders just added. Sew 1" x 42" First Border strips together end-to-end to make one continuous 1"-wide First Border strip. Cut two 1"-wide First Border strips to this measurement. Sew to sides of quilt. Press.

Bravura
Tote

Use left-over blocks and fabric scraps from the lap quilt to create this eye-catching tote. Snap-together curtain grommets add style and allow the tote to open to its full width.

Bravura Tote Bag Approximately: 12" x 16" and 8" deep	FIRST CUT	
	Number of Strips or Pieces	Dimensions
Fabric A Lights Fat Quarter each of 8 Fabrics	3*	5" squares *cut for each fabric
Fabric B Darks Fat Quarter each of 8 Fabrics	3*	5" squares *cut for each fabric
Fabric C Top Accent ¼ yard	1	4½" x 40½"
Fabric D Lining & Handle 1 yard	1 2	21" x 40½" 4½" x 42"
Backing - ⅞ yard (will not show) Batting - 24" x 44" and 1" x 59" Curtain Grommets - 1 Package (8 Grommets)		

Fabric Requirements and Cutting Instructions

Read all instructions before beginning. Use ¼" seam allowance unless noted. Read Cutting Strips and Pieces on page 108 prior to cutting fabric.

Getting Started

This stylish bag is great for any occasion. Block measures 4½" square (unfinished). If using remaining units from Bravura Lap Quilt, skip step 1. Refer to Accurate Seam Allowance on page 108.

Making the Tote

1. Draw a diagonal line on wrong side of one 5" Fabric A square. Place marked square and one 5" Fabric B square right sides together. Sew scant ¼" away from drawn line on both sides to make half-square triangles as shown. Make twenty. Cut on drawn line and press. Square to 4½". This will make forty half-square triangle units.

Fabric A = 5 x 5   Square to 4½
Fabric B = 5 x 5   Make 40
Make 20   Half-square Triangles

2. Arrange and sew together ten units from step 1 as shown. Press. Make four, press seams in opposite direction from row to row.

Make 4
Press seams in opposite direction from row to row

3. Sew rows from step 2 together. Press. Sew one 4½" x 40½" Fabric C strip to top of unit as shown. Press.

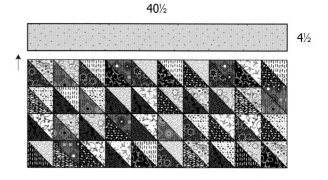

40½

4½

4. Place unit from step 3 on 24" x 44" batting and backing pieces and quilt as desired. Trim batting and backing even with bag edges.

5. Fold tote unit wrong sides together along each fold line indicated in red below. Press to set fold.

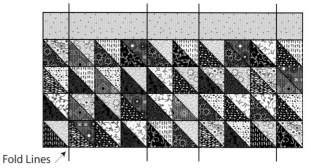

Fold Lines

Finishing the Tote

1. Fold tote unit, right sides together, in half crosswise to make a 20¼" x 20½" folded unit. Sew along side and bottom edges, using ¼"-wide seam. Press seam open.

2. Fold one bottom corner of unit from step 1, matching side seam to bottom seam. Draw an 8"-long line across as shown. Sew on drawn line, anchoring stitches. Repeat for other side.

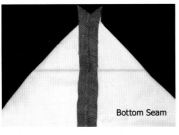

3. Fold stitched corners to bottom seam of tote and tack in place for added stability.

4. Using 21" x 40½" Lining piece, repeat steps 1-3 to make lining insert. Leave a 5" opening along side seam for turning.

5. Turn tote wrong side out. Position and pin lining inside tote, right sides together. Stitch lining and tote together along top edge using a ¼"-wide seam allowance. Turn right side out and press leaving ¼" of lining showing on front side of tote. Hand-stitch opening closed. To form top mock binding, "stitch-in-the-ditch" along seam line of tote and lining, holding lining in place. Top stitch along Fabric C accent strip bottom edge.

6. Refer to manufacturer's instruction to attach eight grommets to top of tote. Measure ⅜" away from each previously pressed fold line, center and trace circles on right side of bag using template provided by manufacturer.

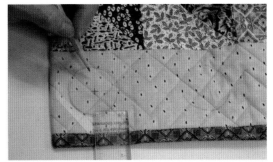

7. Using a narrow zigzag stitch, sew through all layers on drawn circle lines. Following grommet instructions, cut out circles close to stitching. Attach grommets as directed.

8. Sew two 4½" x 42" Fabric D strips end-to-end to make one continuous 4½"-wide strip. Cut strip to measure 4½" x 59".

9. Fold handle strip in half lengthwise, press, and unfold. Bring raw edges to pressed line, press, fold again and press. Unfold piece, insert batting in center and refold strip.

10. Weave handle strip through grommets as shown. Sew handle strap ends together, refold, and press. Topstitch ⅛" away from folded edge on both side of handle.

Color Bar Quilt

Travel half way around the color wheel with this dynamic quilt that vibrates with color energy. Observe how colors come forward or recede depending on color placement and enjoy the bold contemporary design of this striking quilt.

Color Bar Quilt Finished Size: 43" x 57"	FIRST CUT		SECOND CUT	
	Number of Strips or Pieces	Dimensions	Number of Pieces	Dimensions
Fabric A Gold ⅝ yard	1	9½" x 42"	2	9½" x 5½"
			4	9½" x 2½"
			3	6½" x 2½"
	3	2" x 42"	8	2" x 9½"
			8	2" x 2½"
	1	1½" x 42"	4	1½" x 2¼"
			2	1½" squares
			6	1" x 1½"
Fabric B Light Green ½ yard	1	9½" x 42"	3	9½" x 5½"
			3	6½" x 2½"
	2	2" x 42"	6	2" x 9½"
			6	2" x 2½"
			1	1½" square
Fabric C Dark Green ½ yard	1	9½" x 42"	1	9½" x 5½"
			4	9½" x 2½"
			4	6½" x 2½"
	2	2" x 42"	6	2" x 9½"
			6	2" x 2½"
	1	1½" x 42"	4	1½" x 2¼"
			5	1½" squares
			6	1" x 1½"
Fabric D Orange ⅝ yard	1	9½" x 42"	3	9½" x 5½"
			2	9½" x 2½"
			4	6½" x 2½"
	3	2" x 42"	8	2" x 9½"
			8	2" x 2½"
	1	1½" x 42"	2	1½" x 2¼"
			5	1½" squares
			3	1" x 1½"
Fabric E Paprika ½ yard	1	9½" x 42"	3	9½" x 5½"
			2	6½" x 2½"
	2	2" x 42"	6	2" x 9½"
			6	2" x 2½"
	1	1½" x 42"	7	1½" squares

Color Bar Quilt CONTINUED	FIRST CUT		SECOND CUT	
	Number of Strips or Pieces	Dimensions	Number of Pieces	Dimensions
Fabric F Burgundy ½ yard	1	9½" x 42"	2	9½" x 5½"
			2	9½" x 2½"
			4	6½" x 2½"
	2	2" x 42"	6	2" x 9½"
			6	2" x 2½"
	1	1½" x 42"	2	1½" x 2¼"
			4	1½" squares
			3	1" x 1½"
Fabric G Purple ⅝ yard	1	9½" x 42"	3	9½" x 5½"
			2	9½" x 2½"
			4	6½" x 2½"
	3	2" x 42"	8	2" x 9½"
			8	2" x 2½"
	1	1½" x 42"	2	1½" x 2¼"
			4	1½" squares
			3	1" x 1½"
Outside Border ⅓ yard	5	1½" x 42"		
Binding ¼ yard each of 5 Fabrics	2*	2¾" x 42" *cut for each fabric	5*	2¾" x 10½"

Backing - 2⅔ yards
Batting - 47" x 61"

Colorful Concepts

TIP

This quilt, with its rich jewel tones, radiates luxury and warmth and can be made using either cotton or wool. Experiment with colors by making more than one quilt using different color combinations.

Color Bar Quilt
43" x 57"

Fabric Requirements and Cutting Instructions

Read all instructions before beginning and use ¼"-wide seam allowances throughout. Read Cutting Strips and Pieces on page 108 prior to cutting fabric.

Getting Started

Vibrant colors and contemporary design make this quick-sew quilt a stunning addition to your home décor. Blocks measure 5½" x 9½" (unfinished). Refer to Accurate Seam Allowance on page 108. Whenever possible use Assembly Line Method on page 108. Press seams in direction of arrows.

Making the Blocks

Refer to photo on page 49 and layout for fabric combinations used in this quilt.

1. Sew one 6½" x 2½" Fabric G piece between two 2" x 2½" Fabric B pieces. Press seams toward Fabric B. Sew this unit between two matching 2" x 9½" Fabric B strips as shown. Press and label Block 1. Make twenty-four using assorted fabric combinations.

Block 1

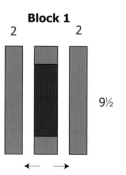

Make 24
(in assorted fabric combinations)
Block measures 5½" x 9½"

Shortcut Construction

This easy-to-construct quilt can be made even easier by fusing smaller rectangles and/or squares to background fabric. For this method, block backgrounds should be cut 5½" x 9½" then either assorted 2" x 6" rectangles or 1" squares fused to blocks. Adjust yardage accordingly.

2. Arrange and sew together two 1½" x 2¼" and three 1" x 1½" Fabric F pieces, and four assorted 1½" squares (Fabric D, A, B, and E are shown). Press.

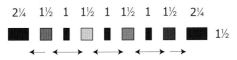

3. Sew unit from step 2 between two 9½" x 2½" Fabric F strips as shown. Press and label Block 2. Make seven using assorted fabric combinations.

Block 2

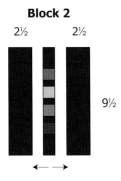

Make 7
(in assorted fabric combinations)
Block measures 5½ x 9½

Assembling the Quilt

1. Refer to photo on page 49 and layout on page 50 to arrange six rows with eight blocks each. All rows, except Row 4, use three assorted 6½" x 9½" rectangles, four of Block 1, and one of Block 2. Row 4 consists of two assorted 6½" x 9½" rectangles, four of Block 1, and two of Block 2.

2. Sew rectangles and blocks into rows. Press seams in opposite direction from row to row. Sew rows together and press.

3. Refer to Adding the Borders on page 110. Sew 1½" x 42" Outside Border strips together end-to-end to make one continuous 1½"-wide Outside Border strip. Measure quilt through center from side to side. Cut two 1½"-wide Outside Border strips to this measurement. Sew to top and bottom of quilt. Press seams toward border.

4. Measure quilt through center from top to bottom including borders just added. Cut two 1½"-wide Outside Border strips to this measurement. Sew to sides of quilt. Press.

Layering and Finishing

1. Cut backing crosswise into two equal pieces. Sew pieces together lengthwise to make one 47" x 80" (approximate) backing piece. Press and trim to 47" x 61".

2. Referring to Layering the Quilt on page 110, arrange and baste backing, batting, and top together. Hand or machine quilt as desired.

3. Refer to Binding the Quilt on page 110. Sew 2¾" x 10½" binding strips end-to-end alternating colors to make one continuous 2¾"-wide binding strip. Bind quilt to finish. Note: Sew binding to top of quilt then right side, bottom, and left side. By using this method, the fabric color wraps around the corners.

> **TIP**
>
> ### Pillow
>
> Decorate a plain purchased pillow with elements from the quilt. Pillow shown below is embellished with ribbons and 1½" fabric squares using the Quick-Fuse Method (page 109). Finish raw edges using a hand blanket stitch, straight stitch or other decorative stitches.

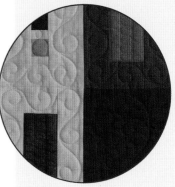

Fun
techniques

Fun Techniques

Think outside the block for a fresh new take on quilting! Strip-piecing makes quilts easy. Paper piecing allows you to create angles and intricate designs. You'll be going in circles with our uncomplicated approach and quilting will become part of the design process when you explore these fun techniques in your next quilts.

Going in Circles Quilt

Pieced circles create an intriguing pattern on this unusual quilt. You'll also be intrigued as this complex-looking quilt (circles!) is actually easy to create with our tips, techniques, and product suggestions.

Going in Circles Quilt Finished Size: 44½" x 56½"	FIRST CUT	
	Number of Strips or Pieces	Dimensions
Fabric A** Light Backgrounds & Circles ⅓ yard 12 Assorted Fabrics	8	9" squares*
	11	7" squares*
	26	5" squares* *cut once diagonally
	4	8" squares
	4	6" squares
	25	4" squares
Fabric B Medium Backgrounds & Circles ⅓ yard 4 Assorted Fabrics	1	9" squares*
	2	7" squares*
	8	5" squares* *cut once diagonally
	2	6" squares
	8	4" squares
Fabric C** Dark Backgrounds & Circles ⅓ yard 8 Assorted Fabrics	7	9" squares*
	6	7" squares*
	16	5" squares* *cut once diagonally
	4	8" squares
	6	6" squares
	16	4" squares
First Border ¼ yard	5	1¼" x 42"
Second Border ¼ yard	5	1½" x 42"
Outside Border ½ yard	5	2½" x 42"
Binding ⅝ yard	6	2¾" x 42"

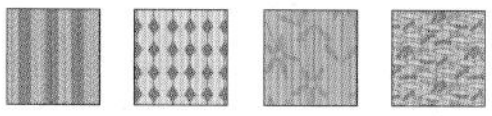

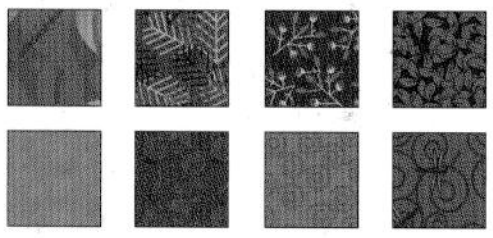

Backing - 2⅞ yards
Batting - 50" x 62"
Misty Fuse™ - 2½ yards

**Note: Cuts listed in chart are the total needed for the project, cut from assorted fabrics. If desired, twenty-four Fat Quarters can be used for Fabric A and C, instead of ⅓ yard, and the project cut from assorted fabrics.

Fabric Requirements and Cutting Instructions

Read all instructions before beginning and use ¼"-wide seam allowances throughout. Read Cutting Strips and Pieces on page 108 prior to cutting fabric.

Getting Started

Simple triangle units in lights and darks make an interesting background for our scrappy pieced circle units. Refer to Accurate Seam Allowance on page 108. Whenever possible use Assembly Line Method on page 108. Press seams in direction of arrows.

Note: When assembling block units, place seam allowances in a counter-clockwise position. After seams are twisted, the seam allowances should all go counter-clockwise. Assemble all blocks in same direction.

TIP

Fun Techniques

The scrappy circles in this quilt are made by first piecing squares. Traced circles are then cut, and appliquéd to blocks. We used Mistyfuse™, (page 111) a very lightweight adhesive that doesn't add stiffness or weight when adhered to the quilt. If you want to use fusible web, trace circles on paper side of fusible web, cut ½" away from both sides of drawn line. This will eliminate the adhesive in center of circle prior to fusing to fabric.

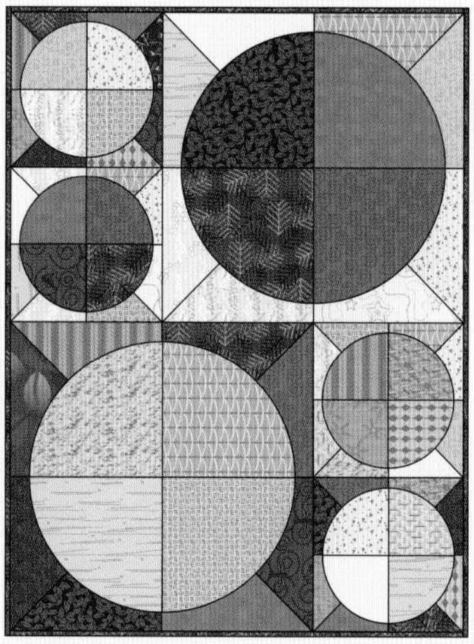

Make it smaller for a delightful wall accent!

Going in Circles Quilt
44½" x 56½"

Making the Blocks

1. Sew two different Fabric A small triangles together as shown. Press. Make twenty-five in assorted fabric combinations. Square to 4½". Sew two units together. Press. Make twelve. Sew two of these units together as shown. Refer to Twisting Seams on page 108 and press. Label units Block 1. Make six in assorted fabric combinations. Block measures 8½" square. Note: Remaining Unit 1 is used in Adding the Circles, step 5.

Block 1

Make 25
(in assorted fabric combinations)
Square to 4½"

Make 6
(in assorted fabric combinations)
Block measures 8½" square

2. Sew two different Fabric B or C small triangles together as shown. Press. Make twenty-four in assorted fabric combinations (B/B, B/C, or C/C). Square to 4½". Sew two units together. Press. Make ten. Sew two of these units together as shown. Twist seams and press. Label units Block 2. Make five in assorted fabric combinations. Block measures 8½" square.

Block 2

Make 24
(in assorted fabric combinations)
Square to 4½"

Make 5
(in assorted fabric combinations)
Block measures 8½" square

3. Sew two remaining units from step 2 together as shown. Press. Make two and label Block 3. Block measures 4½" x 8½".

Block 3

Make 2
(in assorted fabric combinations)
Block measures 4½" x 8½"

4. Sew two different Fabric A medium triangles together as shown. Press. Make eight in assorted fabric combinations. Square to 6½". Sew two units together. Press. Make four. Sew two of these units together as shown. Twist seams and press. Label units Block 4. Make two in assorted fabric combinations. Block measures 12½" square.

Block 4

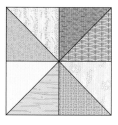

Make 8
(in assorted fabric combinations)
Square to 6½"

Make 2
(in assorted fabric combinations)
Block measures 12½" square

5. Sew two different Fabric B and/or C medium triangles together as shown. Press. Make four in assorted fabric combinations. Square to 6½". Sew two units together. Press. Make two. Sew two of these units together as shown. Twist seams and press. Label units Block 5. Block measures 12½" square.

Block 5

Make 4
(in assorted fabric
combinations)
Square to 6½"

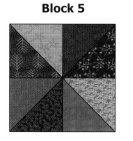

Block measures 12½" square

6. Sew two different Fabric A large triangles together as shown. Press. Make four in assorted fabric combinations. Square to 8½". Sew two units together. Press. Make two. Sew these units together as shown. Twist seams and press. Label units Block 6. Block measures 16½" square.

Block 6

Make 4
(in assorted fabric
combinations)
Square to 8½"

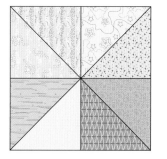

Block measures 16½" square

7. Sew two different Fabric B and/or C large triangles together as shown. Press. Make four in assorted fabric combinations. Square to 8½". Sew two units together. Press. Make two. Sew these units together as shown. Twist seams and press. Label units Block 7. Block measures 16½" square.

Block 7

Make 4
(in assorted fabric
combinations)
Square to 8½"

Block measures 16½" square

8. Refer to photo on page 55 (shown horizontally) and layout on page 56 to arrange all blocks into rows prior to adding the circles to blocks.

Adding the Circles

Refer to appliqué instructions on page 109 and Mistyfuse™ on page 111. Our instructions are for Quick-Fuse Appliqué, but if you prefer hand appliqué, reverse patterns and add ¼"-wide seam allowances.

1. Sew two 4" Fabric B and/or C squares together. Press. Make twelve. Sew two of these units together. Refer to Twisting Seams on page 108 and press. Make six in assorted fabric combination.

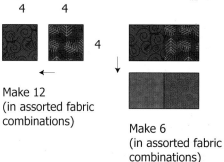

4   4

4

Make 12
(in assorted fabric
combinations)

Make 6
(in assorted fabric
combinations)

2. Use patterns on pages 60-61 to trace eleven Blocks 1 & 2 whole 7" circles, two Block 3 half circles, one Unit 1 quarter circle, three Blocks 4 & 5 whole 10" circles, and two Blocks 6 & 7 whole 13" circles on freezer paper or paper side of lightweight fusible web. Trace placement lines on whole circle patterns. Use appropriate fabrics to prepare all appliqués for fusing.

3. Align small circle blue placement lines with Block 1 seam lines. Refer to manufacturer's instructions to fuse 7" circle to one Block 1 as shown. Make six.

Block 1

Make 6

4. Repeat steps 1 and 3 to fuse 7" circles (four 4" Fabric A squares) to five of Block 2.

Block 2

Make 5
(in assorted fabric
combinations)

Make 5

5. Repeat steps 1 and 3 to sew, press, and fuse half-circles (two 4" Fabric A squares) to two of Block 3. Fuse quarter-circle (4" Fabric A square) to Unit 1. Sew one Block 3 to Unit 1 as shown. Press and relabel as Block 3.

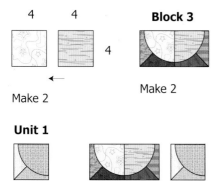

Make 2

Make 2

Unit 1

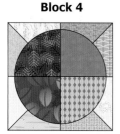

6. Repeat steps 1 and 3 to sew, press, and fuse 10" circles (four 6" Fabric C squares) to two of Block 4, 10" circles (four 6" Fabric A squares) to one Block 5, 13" circle (four 8" Fabric C squares) to one Block 6, and 13" circle (four 8" Fabric A squares) to one Block 7.

Block 4   **Block 5**

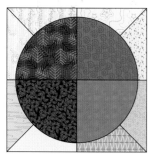

Make 2

Block 6   **Block 7**

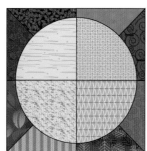

7. Finish all appliqué edges with machine zigzag stitch, satin stitch or other decorative stitching as desired.

Assembling the Quilt

Refer to photo on page 55 and layout on page 56 for all steps.

1. Sew one Block 1 to one Block 2. Press seams toward Block 2. Make five and label Block 1/2.

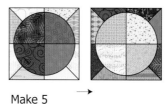

Make 5

2. Sew one Block 3 to one Block 4 as shown. Press. Sew one Block 7 between one Block 1/2 and Block 3/4 from this step. Press.

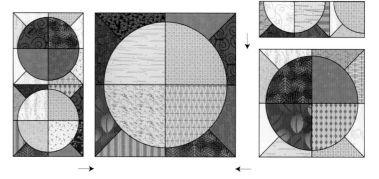

3. Sew two Block 1/2 together as shown. Press. Sew one Block 6 to top of unit. Press.

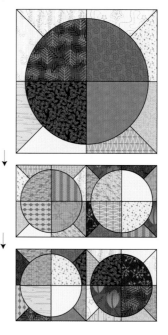

4. Sew one Block 1/2 to one Block 3 as shown Press.

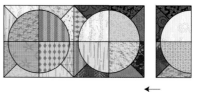

5. Sew one Block 5 to one Block 4 as shown. Press.

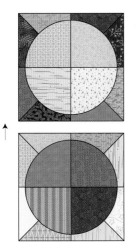

6. Sew one Block 1/2 to one Block 1 as shown Press. Sew unit from step 5 to this unit. Press. Sew unit from step 4 to top of unit from this step. Press.

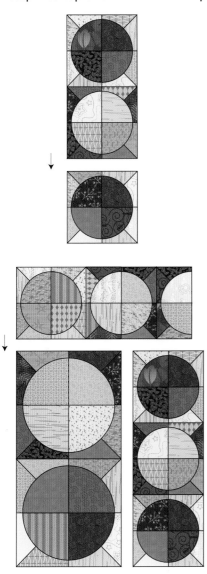

7. Referring to photo on page 55 and layout on page 56, sew unit from step 3 to unit from step 6. Press. Sew unit from step 2 to top of unit from this step. Press.

Adding the Borders

1. Refer to Adding the Borders on page 110. Measure quilt through center from side to side. Cut two 1¼"-wide First Border strips to this measurement. Sew to top and bottom of quilt. Press seams toward border.

2. Sew 1¼" x 42" First Border strips together end-to-end to make one continuous 1¼"-wide First Border strip. Measure quilt through center from top to bottom including borders just added. Cut two 1¼"-wide First Border strips to this measurement. Sew to sides of quilt. Press.

3. Refer to steps 1 and 2 to join, measure, trim, and sew 1½"-wide Second Border strips and 2½"-wide Outside Border strips to top, bottom, and sides of quilt. Press.

Layering and Finishing

1. Cut backing crosswise into two equal pieces. Sew pieces together lengthwise to make one 51" x 80" (approximate) backing piece. Press and trim to 51" x 62".

2. Referring to Layering the Quilt on page 110, arrange and baste backing, batting, and top together. Hand or machine quilt as desired.

3. Refer to Binding the Quilt on page 110. Sew 2¾" x 42" binding strips end-to-end to make one continuous 2¾"-wide binding strip. Bind quilt to finish.

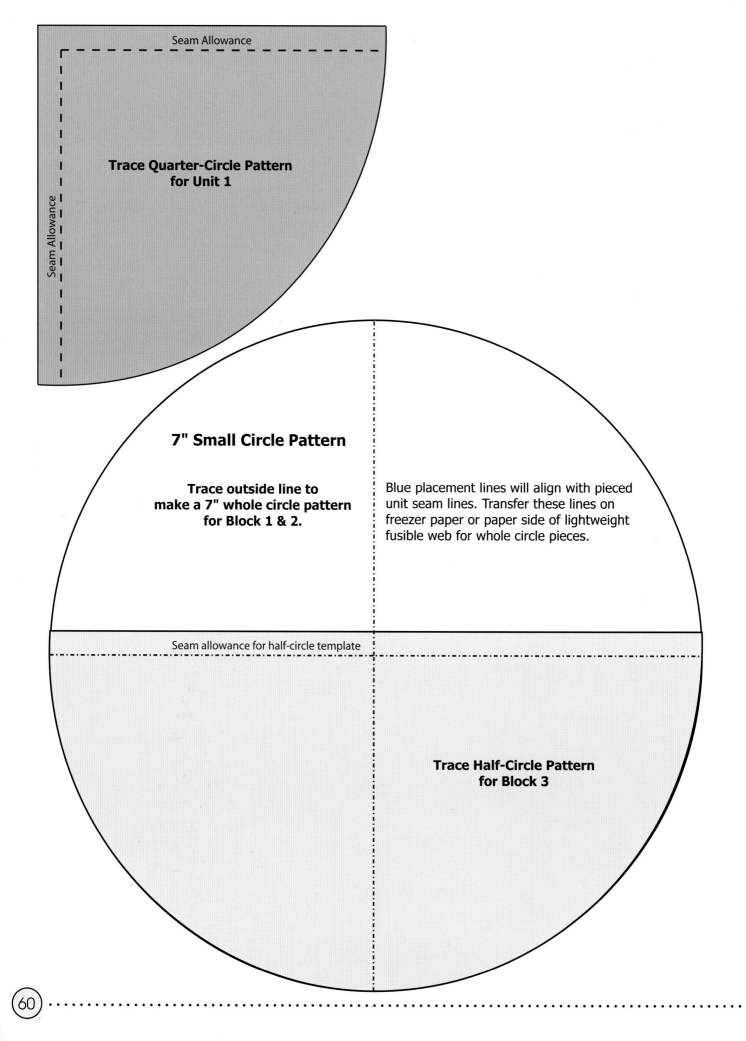

**Trace Quarter-Circle Pattern
for Unit 1**

Seam Allowance

Seam Allowance

7" Small Circle Pattern

**Trace outside line to
make a 7" whole circle pattern
for Block 1 & 2.**

Blue placement lines will align with pieced
unit seam lines. Transfer these lines on
freezer paper or paper side of lightweight
fusible web for whole circle pieces.

Seam allowance for half-circle template

**Trace Half-Circle Pattern
for Block 3**

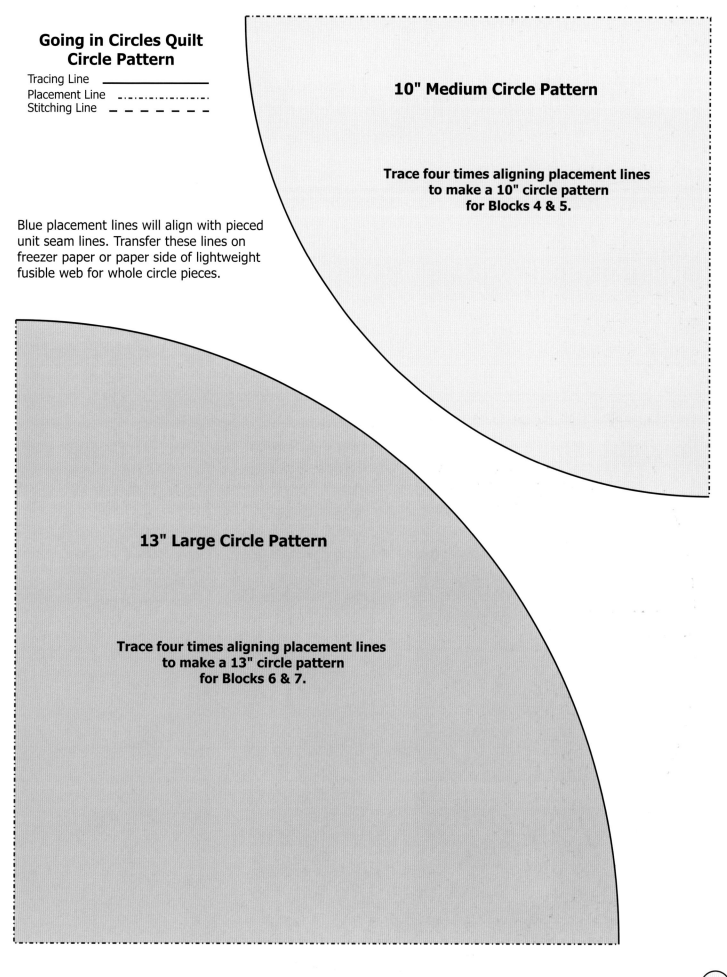

Going in Circles Quilt
Circle Pattern

Tracing Line
Placement Line
Stitching Line

Blue placement lines will align with pieced unit seam lines. Transfer these lines on freezer paper or paper side of lightweight fusible web for whole circle pieces.

10" Medium Circle Pattern

**Trace four times aligning placement lines
to make a 10" circle pattern
for Blocks 4 & 5.**

13" Large Circle Pattern

**Trace four times aligning placement lines
to make a 13" circle pattern
for Blocks 6 & 7.**

Strips 'n Stripes Lap Quilt

Strip-pieced sets create beautiful bars of color on this fast and fun lap quilt. Colors inspired by nature give the quilt easy-on-the-eyes ambiance. Simple settings and different block sizes and directions highlight the strip-pieced stripes.

Strips 'n Stripes Lap Quilt Finished Size: 42" x 59"	FIRST CUT		SECOND CUT	
	Number of Strips or Pieces	Dimensions	Number of Pieces	Dimensions
Fabric A Block 1 Background ⅜ yard	2	5¼" x 42"	12	5¼" squares* *cut once diagonally
Fabric B Block 2 Background ⅜ yard	2	5¼" x 42"	12	5¼" squares* *cut once diagonally
Fabric C Block 1 Center ⅙ yard each of 8 Fabrics	3**	1¼" x 42" **cut for each fabric	2**	1¼" x 6½"
Fabric D Block 2 Center ⅛ yard each of 8 Fabrics	2**	1¼" x 42" **cut for each fabric		
Fabric E Block 3 Border ⅓ yard	1 3	2¼" x 42" 1¾" x 42"	6 6	2¼" x 6½" 1¾" x 17½"
Fabric F Block 4 Border ⅓ yard	1 3	2¼" x 42" 1¾" x 42"	6 6	2¼" x 6½" 1¾" x 17½"
First Border ¼ yard	5	1¼" x 42"		
Second Border ¼ yard	5	1¼" x 42"		
Outside Border ½ yard	5	2½" x 42"		
Binding ⅝ yard	6	2¾" x 42"		
Backing - 2⅔ yards Batting - 48" x 65"				

Fabric Requirements and Cutting Instructions

Read all instructions before beginning and use ¼"-wide seam allowances throughout. Read Cutting Strips and Pieces on page 108 prior to cutting fabric.

Getting Started

Have fun tossing and turning these blocks adding interest to an awesomely simple unit. Blocks measure 9" x 17½" (unfinished). Refer to Accurate Seam Allowance on page 108. Whenever possible use Assembly Line Method on page 108. Press seams in direction of arrows.

Making the Blocks

1. Sew together eight different 1¼" x 42" Fabric C strips as shown to make a strip set. Press seams in one direction. Make two. Cut strips into twelve 6½"-wide segments as shown.

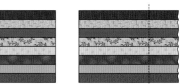

6½

Make 2
Cut 12 segments

Fun Techniques

This quilt uses strip piecing, which is an easier, faster, and more accurate way of sewing multiple strips together to make a unit. It is especially important when sewing multiple pieces together to use an accurate seam allowance. Refer to page 108 for a simple test to check for accuracy.

TIP

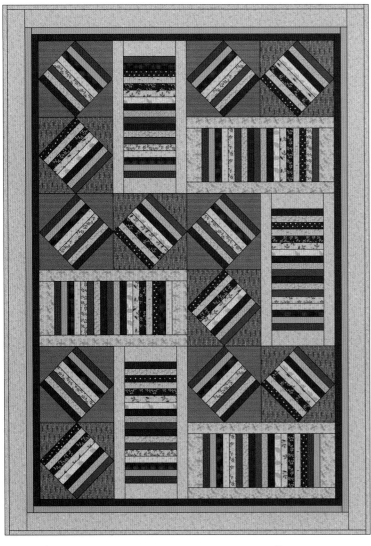

Strips 'n Stripes Lap Quilt
42" x 59"

3. Sew together eight different 1¼" x 42" Fabric D strips as shown to make a strip set. Press seams in one direction. Make two. Cut strips into twelve 6½"-wide segments as shown.

6½

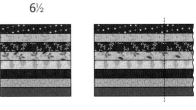

Make 2
Cut 12 segments

4. Sew four Fabric B triangles to one unit from step 3 as shown. Triangle ends will extend past block edges. Press. Make six and label Block 2. Square unit to 9".

Block 2

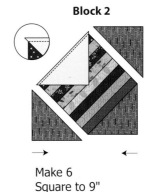

Make 6
Square to 9"

5. Refer to photo on page 63 and layout to check orientation of blocks prior to sewing. Sew one Block 1 to one Block 2. Press. Make six. Block measures 9" x 17½".

Block 1/2

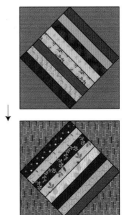

Make 6
Block measures 9" x 17½"

2. Sew four Fabric A triangles to one unit from step 1 as shown. Triangle ends will extend past block edges. Press. Make six and label Block 1. Square unit to 9".

Block 1

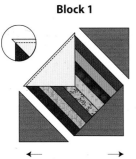

Make 6
Square to 9"

6. Sew two different 1¼" x 6½" Fabric C pieces to one Block 1 center unit and one Block 2 center unit as shown. Press. Make six.

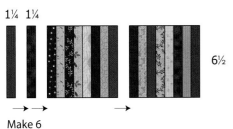

1¼ 1¼

6½

Make 6

7. Sew one unit from step 6 between two 2¼" x 6½" Fabric E pieces. Press seams toward Fabric E. Sew this unit between two 1¾" x 17½" Fabric E strips as shown. Press. Make three and label Block 3. Block measures 9" x 17½".

Block 3

1¾ 1¾

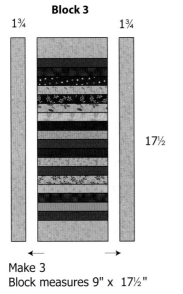

17½

Make 3
Block measures 9" x 17½"

8. Sew one unit from step 6 between two 2¼" x 6½" Fabric F pieces. Press seams toward Fabric F. Sew this unit between two 1¾" x 17½" Fabric F strips as shown. Press. Make three and label Block 4. Block measures 9" x 17½".

Block 4

1¾ 1¾

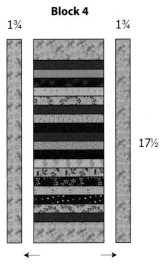

17½

Make 3
Block measures 9" x 17½"

Assembling the Quilt

1. Referring to photo on page 63 and layout on page 64, arrange all blocks as shown, paying close attention to block orientation.

2. Sew one Block 1/2 to one Block 3. Press. Make three. Sew one Block 1/2 to one Block 4. Press. Make three.

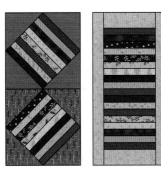

Make 3

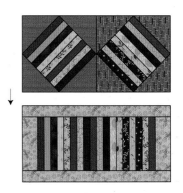

Make 3

3. Referring to photo on page 63 and layout on page 64, arrange blocks from step 2 into three rows with two blocks each. Sew blocks into rows. Press seams in opposite direction from row to row. Sew rows together. Press.

Adding the Borders

1. Refer to Adding the Borders on page 110. Measure quilt through center from side to side. Cut two 1¼"-wide First Border strips to this measurement. Sew to top and bottom of quilt. Press seams toward border.

2. Sew 1¼" x 42" First Border strips together end-to-end to make one continuous 1¼"-wide First Border strip. Measure quilt through center from top to bottom including borders just added. Cut two 1¼"-wide First Border strips to this measurement. Sew to sides of quilt. Press.

3. Refer to steps 1 and 2 to join, measure, trim, and sew 1¼"-wide Second Border strips, and 2½"-wide Outside Border strips to top, bottom, and sides of quilt. Press.

Layering and Finishing

1. Cut backing crosswise into two equal pieces. Sew pieces together lengthwise to make one 48" x 80" (approximate) backing piece. Press and trim to 48" x 65".

2. Referring to Layering the Quilt on page 110, arrange and baste backing, batting, and top together. Hand or machine quilt as desired.

3. Refer to Binding the Quilt on page 110. Sew 2¾" x 42" binding strips end-to-end to make one continuous 2¾"-wide binding strip. Bind quilt to finish.

Thread Design
Pillows

The design focus is on thread and various quilting and embroidery techniques on these three decorator pillows. Simple piecing sets the scene for thread embellishment and wide flanges in print fabrics frame the handiwork. Try these same techniques on your next quilt.

Fabric Requirements and Cutting Instructions

Read all instructions before beginning and use ¼"-wide seam allowances throughout. Read Cutting Strips and Pieces on page 108 prior to cutting fabric.

Getting Started

These three simple pillows each use a different quilting technique: an all-over quilting design using variegated threads, big-stitch hand quilting, and double-stitch or triple-stitch quilting by machine. Pillows finish 18" square.

Making the Big-Stitch Pillow Top

1. Referring to photo, arrange and sew together two 3" x 14½" Fabric A strips, two 3½" x 14½" Fabric A strips, and three 1½" x 14½" Fabric B strips. Press seams toward Fabric A.

2. Sew unit from step 1 between two 2½" x 14½" Outside Border strips. Press seams toward border. Sew this unit between two 2½" x 18½" Outside Border strips. Press.

3. Refer to Big-Stitch Flower pattern on page 68 and pillow photo. Using fabric removable markers, trace flowers to pillow top. Note: Our pillow has one whole flower and three partial flowers.

4. Refer to Finishing Pillows on page 111, step 1, to prepare pillow top for quilting. If combining machine quilting and Big Stitch Technique, complete machine quilting first. To make a Big Stitch, use embroidery needle with number 8 crochet thread, perle cotton, or three strands of embroidery floss. Anchor the knot in batting as in hand quilting. Make ¼"-long stitches on top and ⅛"-long stitches underneath, so large stitches stand out. Refer to page 67 for Finishing the Pillow.

SUPPLIES

Fabric A - Background ¼ yard
    Two 3½" x 14½"
    Two 3" x 14½"
Fabric B - Accent ⅙ yard
    Three 1½" x 14½"
Outside Border ¼ yard
    Two 2½" x 18½"
    Two 2½" x 14½"
Backing - ½ yard
Batting & Lining - 22" x 22"
Pillow Form - 16"
Crochet Thread, Perle Cotton or Embroidery Floss

Big Stitch

Making the Double Stitch Pillow Top

1. Referring to photo, sew 6½" Fabric A square between two 2" x 6½" First Border pieces. Press seams toward border. Sew this unit between two 2" x 9½" First Border pieces. Press.

2. Sew unit from step 1 between two 1½" x 9½" Second Border strips. Press seams toward border just sewn. Sew this unit between two 1½" x 11½" Second Border strips. Press.

3. Sew unit from step 2 between two 2" x 11½" Third Border strips. Press seams toward border just sewn. Sew this unit between two 2" x 14½" Third border strips. Press.

4. Sew unit from step 3 between two 2½" x 14½" Outside Border strips. Press seams toward border just sewn. Sew this unit between two 2½" x 18½" Outside Border strips. Press.

5. Refer to quilting pattern on page 69 and use fabric removable marker to trace pattern on pillow top.

6. Refer to Finishing Pillows on page 111, step 1, to prepare pillow top for quilting. Use a dark brown thread for stems and a contrasting green thread for leaves. Quilt on drawn lines going over design elements twice to add dimension. Note: If machine has a triple stitch feature, use it instead, and go over design elements once. Refer to Finishing the Pillows for flange and backing instructions.

SUPPLIES

Fabric A - Center Scrap
    One 6½" square
First Border - ⅛ yard
    Two 2" x 9½"
    Two 2" x 6½"
Second Border - ⅛ yard
    Two 1½" x 11½"
    Two 1½" x 9½"
Third Border - ⅙ yard
    Two 2" x 14½"
    Two 2" x 11½"
Outside Border - ¼ yard
    Two 2½" x 18½"
    Two 2½" x 14½"
Backing - ½ yard
Batting & Lining - 22" x 22"
Pillow Form - 16"
Contrasting Threads

Making the Variegated Pillow Top

1. Sew 7½" Fabric A square between two 2" x 7½" Fabric B strips. Press seams toward Fabric B. Sew this unit between two 2" x 10½" Fabric B strips. Press.

2. Sew Fabric C triangles to unit from step 1. Press seams toward triangles. Note: Triangle ends extend past unit edge.

3. Sew unit from step 2 between two 2½" x 14½" Outside Border strips. Press seams toward border. Sew this unit between two 2½" x 18½" Outside Border strips. Press.

4. Refer to Finishing Pillows on page 111, step 1, to prepare pillow top for quilting. Select an all over repeating design and quilt center of pillow using a variegated thread. Refer to Finishing the Pillows below.

SUPPLIES

Fabric A - Center Scrap
    One 7½" square
Fabric B - Accent ⅛ yard
    Two 2" x 10½"
    Two 2" x 7½"
Fabric C - Triangles ⅓ yard
    Two 8" squares*
    *Cut once diagonally
Outside Border - ¼ yard
    Two 2½" x 18½"
    Two 2½" x 14½"
Backing - ½ yard
Batting & Lining - 22" x 22"
Pillow Form - 16"
Variegated Thread

Finishing the Pillows

1. Cut two 12" x 18½" backing pieces and refer to Finishing Pillows, page 111, steps 2-4, to sew backing.

2. To create a pillow flange, turn pillow right side out and press. Stitch-in-the-ditch through all layers on outside border seam. Center of pillow measures 16". Quilt Outside Border as desired.

3. Insert 16" pillow form or refer to Pillow Forms page 111 to make a pillow form if desired.

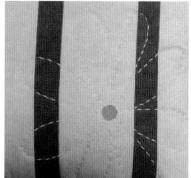

Thread Design Pillows
Big Stitch Pillow Pattern

Tracing Line ————————

Placement Line _._._._._._._._._

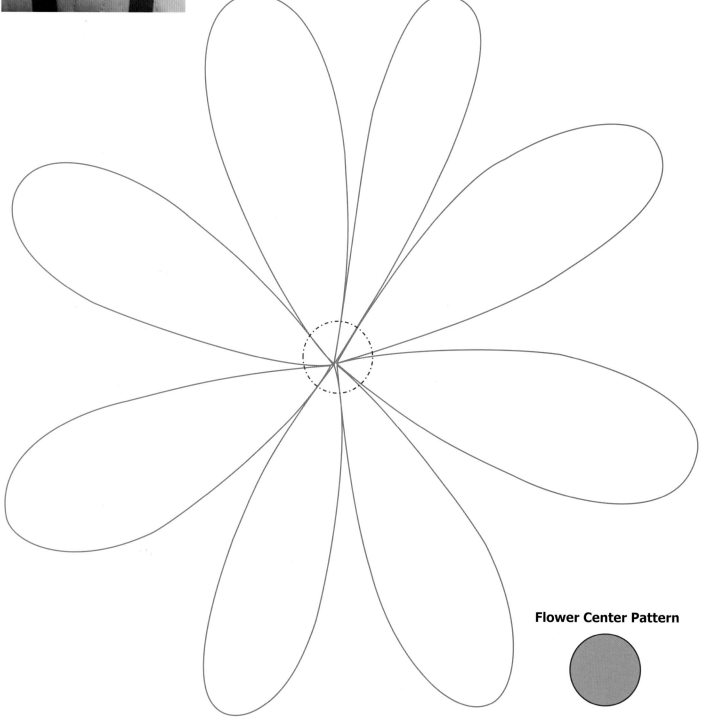

Flower Center Pattern

Thread Design Pillows
Double Stitch Pillow Pattern

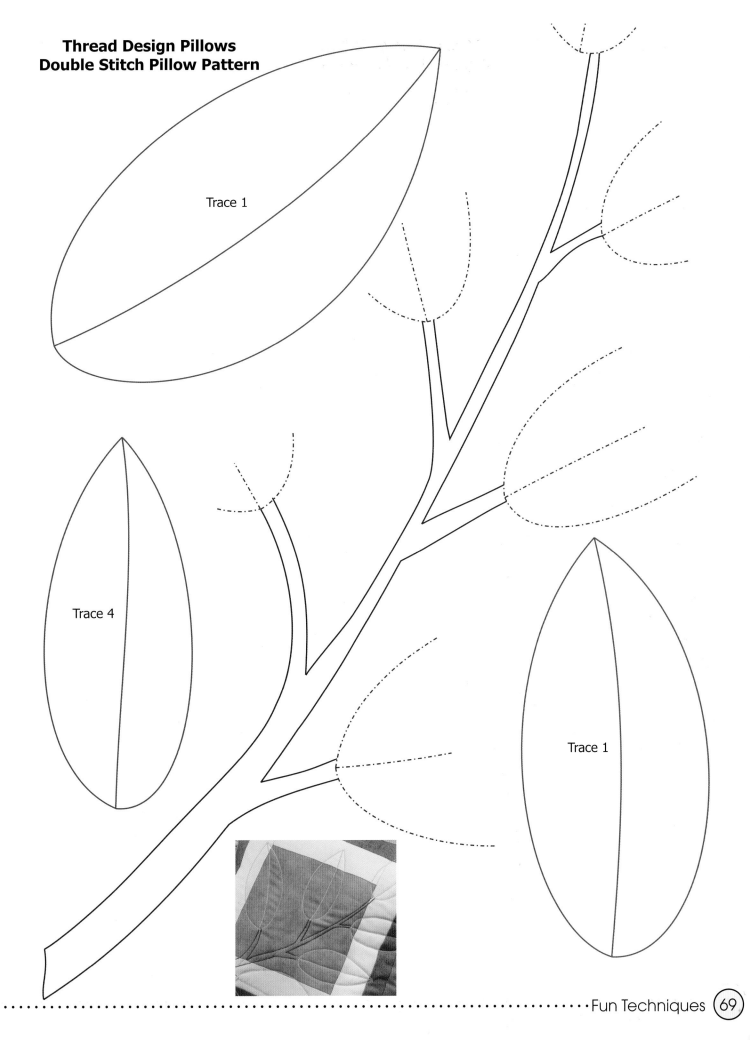

Trace 1

Trace 4

Trace 1

Floating Petals
Lap Quilt

Petals float on a green sea, some rising on the waves and some floating on the surface on this quilt where the trapunto quilting technique is essential to the design. Strip-piecing makes the tonal background quick and easy.

Floating Petals Lap Quilt Finished Size: 46½" x 56½"	FIRST CUT	
	Number of Strips or Pieces	Dimensions
Fabric A Background ½ yard each of 7 Fabrics	5*	2½" x 42" *cut for each fabric
First Border ¼ yard	5	1¼" x 42"
Outside Border ½ yard	5	2½" x 42"
Appliqué Petals Fat Quarter each of 4 Fabrics		
Binding ⅝ yard	6	2¾" x 42"
Backing - 3 yards **Batting - 53" x 64"**** ****Trapunto Quilting requires two different battings. See Fun Technique for information.**		

Fabric Requirements and Cutting Instructions

Read all instructions before beginning and use ¼"-wide seam allowances throughout. Read Cutting Strips and Pieces on page 108 prior to cutting fabric.

Getting Started

Flower petals are scattered against a field of multi-shaded green background fabrics. Block measures 10½" square (unfinished). Refer to Accurate Seam Allowance on page 108. Whenever possible use Assembly Line Method on page 108. Press seams in direction of arrows.

Making the Blocks

1. Cut each 2½" x 42" Fabric A strip in half to make two 2½" x 21" strips.

Fun Technique

TIP

Trapunto quilting is a stuffing technique that adds texture and dimension to quilting. There are different ways to accomplish the dimensional look. One method is suggested below. Check local quilt shops and the Internet for other methods.

1. Select a closed quilting design like feathers, ovals, hearts, or repeat the block subject design as we did on this quilt. Using fabric removable marker, trace design on quilt top.

2. Layer and baste backing, regular batting (80/20-cotton or something similar), medium to high loft polyester batting, and quilt top together. Note: You can add more layers of loftier batting under certain design areas. This adds extra loft to the trapunto.

3. Set machine for free motion quilting. Quilt on all marked lines.

4. Fill in background area using a tight stitch design like a meandering stitch, echo stitching or a tight grid design. The background stitch will flatten the area around the stuffed quilt design.

Floating Petals Lap Quilt
46½" x 56½"

2. Sew together five assorted 2½" x 21" Fabric A strips to make a strip set. Press seams in one direction. Make thirteen in assorted combinations. Cut strip sets into one hundred 2½"-wide segments as shown.

2½

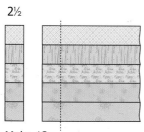

Make 13
in assorted combinations
Cut 100 segments

3. When piecing the block, rotate strip sets so seams go in opposite direction from strip to strip as shown.

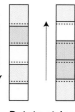

Rotate strips for
opposing seams

4. Arrange and sew together five strip sets from step 2 as shown. Press. Block measure 10½" square. Make twenty in assorted combinations.

Make 20
in assorted combinations

Adding the Appliqués

Refer to appliqué instructions on page 109. Our instructions are for Quick-Fuse Appliqué, but if you prefer hand appliqué add ¼"-wide seam allowances.

1. Use pattern on page 73 to trace forty-eight petals on paper side of fusible web. Use appropriate fabrics to prepare all appliqués for fusing. Note: Four matching petals are used for each of twelve blocks. We used four different fabrics making three blocks of each.

2. Refer to photo on page 71 and layout to position and fuse appliqués to blocks. Finish appliqué edges with machine satin stitch or other decorative stitching as desired.

Assembling the Quilt

1. Referring to photo on page 71 and layout on page 72 to arrange and sew together five rows with four blocks each. Press seams in opposite direction from row to row.

2. Sew rows together. Press.

Adding the Borders

1. Refer to Adding the Borders on page 110. Sew 1¼" x 42" First Border strips together end-to-end to make one continuous 1¼"-wide First Border strip. Measure quilt through center from side to side. Cut two 1¼"-wide First Border strips to this measurement. Sew to top and bottom of quilt. Press seams toward border.

2. Measure quilt through center from top to bottom including borders just added. Cut two 1¼"-wide First Border strips to this measurement. Sew to sides of quilt. Press.

3. Refer to steps 1 and 2 to join, measure, trim, and sew 2½"-wide Outside Border strips to top, bottom, and sides of quilt. Press.

Layering and Finishing

1. Cut backing crosswise into two equal pieces. Sew pieces together lengthwise to make one 54" x 80" (approximate) backing piece. Press and trim to 54" x 64".

2. Referring to Layering the Quilt on page 110, arrange and baste backing, batting, and top together. Hand or machine quilt as desired. Note: Our quilt used a trapunto quilting technique. Refer to Trapunto Tip Box on page 70 to add quilting detail to quilt.

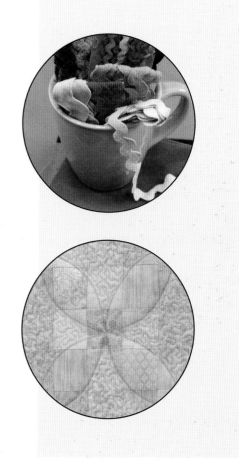

Trapunto & Appliqué Petal Pattern
Make 48

Tip a Canoe
Lap Quilt

Experiment with paper piecing to create these striking blocks for a graphic and handsome lap quilt. Paper piecing is time-consuming but gives you accurate results. The blue color weaves in and out on this quilt adding another visual dimension.

Tip a Canoe Lap Quilt Finished Size: 44" x 56"	FIRST CUT		SECOND CUT	
	Number of Strips or Pieces	Dimensions	Number of Pieces	Dimensions
Fabric A Light Tans ½ yard each of 6 Fabrics	2*	4½" x 42"	8*	4½" x 8½" (#2 & #3)
			4*	4½" x 2½" (#4)
	1*	4" x 42" *cut for each fabric	4*	4" x 8" (#1)
Fabric B Dark Browns ⅓ yard each of 6 Fabrics	2*	4½" x 42" *cut for each fabric	8*	4½" x 8½" (#2 & #3)
			4*	4½" x 2½" (#4)
Fabric C Dark Blues ⅙ yard each of 6 Fabrics	1*	4" x 42" **cut for each fabric	4*	4" x 8" (#1)
First Border ⅓ yard	5	1½" x 42"		
Second Border ¼ yard	5	1" x 42"		
Outside Border ½ yard	5	2½" x 42"		
Binding ⅝ yard	6	2¾" x 42"		
Backing - 2⅞ yards Batting - 50" x 62" Flower-Head Pins				

Fabric Requirements and Cutting Instructions

Read all instructions before beginning and use ¼"-wide seam allowances throughout. Read Cutting Strips and Pieces on page 108 prior to cutting fabric.

Getting Started

Sewing points are a snap when making these simple paper-pieced units. Block measures 12½" square (unfinished). Refer to Accurate Seam Allowance on page 108. Whenever possible use Assembly Line Method on page 108. Press seams in direction of arrows.

TIP

Fun Techniques

Paper piecing is a great technique when sewing odd shaped units, elongated triangles, or multi-piece blocks together. It uses a fold, flip, cut, and sew method. The Add-A-Quarter tool makes the job easier. The lip on this ruler automatically allows for a ¼"-wide seam allowance. Similar rulers on the market are the Add An-Eighth ruler for miniatures, and Add Three-Eighths ruler for foundation piecing with flannel fabric.

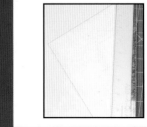

Tip a Canoe Lap Quilt
44" x 56"

Making the Blocks

Refer to paper-piecing pattern on page 78. Forty-eight copies are needed for this project. It is recommended to make a few extra copies. Make all copies from the same copier to avoid distortion. Trim pattern ½" away from outside pattern edge. Units will be trimmed on outside trim line after units are sewn together.

1. Place wrong side of fabric to wrong side of printed pattern, centering 4" x 8" Fabric C #1 piece over section #1. Pin using a flower-head pin, keeping pin away from stitch lines. If necessary, hold pieces up to light to make sure Fabric C extends past section #1 shape.

2. Using a card stock or file folder to aid in folding paper, fold paper along stitch line between sections #1 and #2 as shown. Align ruler ¼" from folded paper edge and trim fabric as shown.

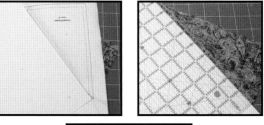

3. Unfold paper, align 4½" x 8½" Fabric A #2 piece on Fabric C cut edge from step 1, right sides together, as shown. Pin in place. Once confidence with this technique increases, pieces can be held in place by hand instead of pinning.

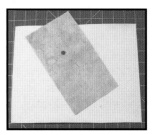

4. Turn paper printed side up, being careful not to displace fabric on back, sew through all layers along Section #1/2 stitch line, using a short stitch length (14"-20" per inch). Begin and end stitches ¼" beyond stitch line. Press.

5. Repeat process to sew the following to unit; 4½" x 8½" Fabric A #3 piece to section #3, and 4½" x 2½" Fabric A #4 piece to section #4 as shown.

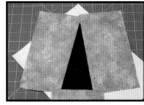

6. After all sections are sewn, press and trim piece on outside trim line to measure 6½" x 6½".

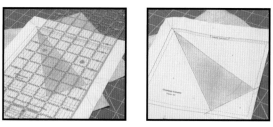

7. Repeat steps 1-6 to make a total of twenty-four paper pieced units, four of each combination as shown.

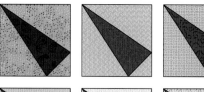

Make 24
(4 of each combination)

8. Repeat steps 1-6 to make a total of twenty-four paper-pieced units, four of each combination as shown. Use 4½" x 8½" Fabric B #2 and #3 pieces, 4½" x 2½" Fabric B #4 pieces, and 4" x 8" Fabric A #1 pieces.

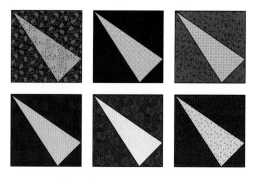

Make 24
(4 of each combination)

9. Sew one unit from step 7 to one unit from step 8 matching Fabric A. Press. Make four.

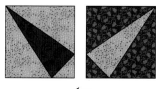

Make 4

10. Sew two units from step 9 together as shown. Refer to Twisting Seams on page 108 and press. Make two.

Make 2

11. Refer to steps 7-9 to make two of each combination as shown. Blocks measures 12½" square.

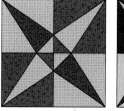

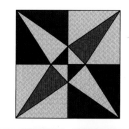

Make 2 of each combination

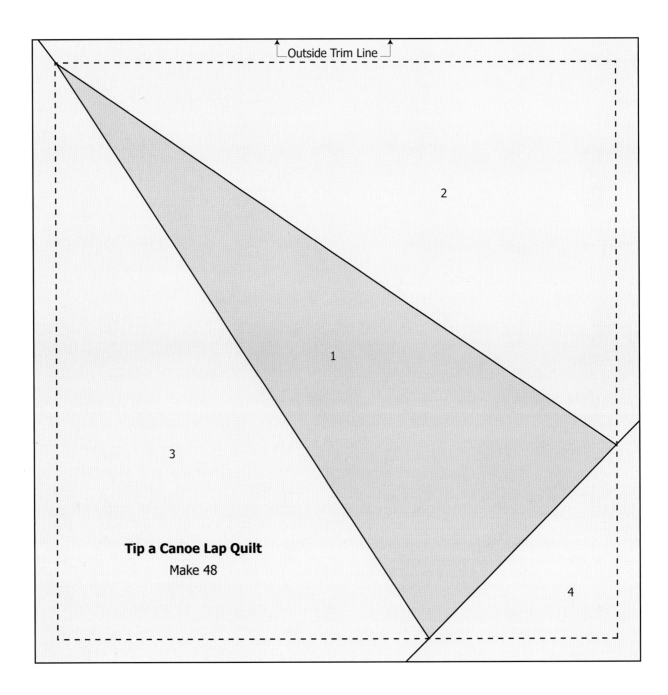

Outside Trim Line

2

1

3

Tip a Canoe Lap Quilt
Make 48

4

Tip a Canoe Lap Quilt Paper Piecing Pattern

48 copies are needed for this project.
It is recommended to make a few extra copies.

*Permission is granted by Debbie Mumm® to copy page 78 to successfully
complete the Tip a Canoe Lap Quilt. Compare copy to the original.
Copy should measure 6½" x 6½". Adjust copier settings if it varies.*

Assembling the Quilt

1. Referring to photo on page 75 and layout on page 76, arrange and sew four rows with three blocks each. Press rows in opposite direction from row to row.

2. Sew rows together. Press.

Adding the Borders

1. Refer to Adding the Borders on page 110. Measure quilt through center from side to side. Cut two 1½"-wide First Border strips to this measurement. Sew to top and bottom of quilt. Press seams toward border.

2. Sew 1½" x 42" First Border strips together end-to-end to make one continuous 1½"-wide First Border strip. Measure quilt through center from top to bottom including borders just added. Cut two 1½"-wide First Border strips to this measurement. Sew to sides of quilt. Press.

3. Refer to steps 1 and 2 to join, measure, trim, and sew 1"-wide Second Border strips, and 2½"-wide Outside Border strips to top, bottom, and sides of quilt. Press.

Layering and Finishing

1. Cut backing crosswise into two equal pieces. Sew pieces together lengthwise to make one 51" x 80" (approximate) backing piece. Press and trim to 51" x 62".

2. Referring to Layering the Quilt on page 110, arrange and baste backing, batting, and top together. Hand or machine quilt as desired.

3. Refer to Binding the Quilt on page 110. Sew 2¾" x 42" binding strips end-to-end to make one continuous 2¾"-wide binding strip. Bind quilt to finish.

Appliqué & embellishments

Appliqué & Embellishments

Beauty is in the details in this charming collection of quilts that focus on appliqué and embellishment techniques. Learn how buttons, beads, and embroidery, as well as couched yarn, decorative stitching, and carefully considered quilting can make your quilts extraordinary.

Flights of Fancy
Wall Quilt

Appliquéd owls are teamed with rotating pinwheels on this sweet and fanciful wall quilt. Circular quilting on the pinwheels gives them movement and positioning of the owls' eyes adds humor and charm to this quaint quilt.

Flights of Fancy Wall Quilt Finished Size: 28½" x 28½"	FIRST CUT		SECOND CUT	
	Number of Strips or Pieces	Dimensions	Number of Pieces	Dimensions
Fabric A Background ⅓ yard	1	8½" x 42"	3	8½" x 12½"
Fabric B Owl Block Triangles Obese Eighth each of 3 Fabrics	2*	5" x 7" *cut for each fabric		
Fabric C Large Pinwheel Light Obese Eighth each of 3 Fabrics	2*	5" squares *cut for each fabric		
Fabric D Large Pinwheel Dark Obese Eighth each of 3 Fabrics	2*	5" squares *cut for each fabric		
Fabric E Small Pinwheel Light ⅛ yard	1	3" x 42"	12	3" squares
Fabric F Small Pinwheel Dark Obese Eighth each of 3 Fabrics	4*	3" squares *cut for each fabric		
First Border ⅙ yard	4	1" x 42"	2 2	1" x 25½" 1" x 24½"
Outside Border ⅞ yard	1	28½" x 42"	1 2 1	28½" x 2" 27" x 2" 25½" x 2"
Binding ⅓ yard	4	2¼" x 42" ¼" Finished Binding		

Appliqués - Assorted scraps
Backing - 1 yard
Batting - 33" x 33"
Lightweight Fusible Web - ½ yard

Freezer Paper

Fabric Requirements and Cutting Instructions

Read all instructions before beginning and use ¼"-wide seam allowances throughout. Read Cutting Strips and Pieces on page 108 prior to cutting fabric.

Getting Started

Simple block construction using colorful fabrics adds a whimsical element to this quilt. Blocks measure 8½" x 10½", 8½" square, and 4½" square (unfinished). Refer to Accurate Seam Allowance on page 108. Whenever possible use Assembly Line Method on page 108. Press seams in direction of arrows.

Making the Owl Blocks

Refer to appliqué instructions on page 109. Our owl instructions are for Quick-Fuse Appliqué, but if you prefer hand appliqué, reverse patterns and add ¼"-wide seam allowances.

Flights of Fancy Wall Quilt
28½" x 28½"

1. Refer to page 86 for triangle patterns. Trace two of each triangle pattern on paper side of freezer paper.

2. Align one paper triangle on one 5" x 7" Fabric B piece, wrong sides together as shown. Press. (Freezer paper will remain in place after pressing.) Align another matching triangle to opposite corner and press. (Triangle angled edge is the sewing line.) Press remaining two triangle pieces to one 5" x 7" matching Fabric B piece. Trim excess fabric along right angle sides of triangle edges even with paper. **Cut ¼" away from pattern angle edge to allow for seam allowance.**

Trim ¼" away from angle edge (noted in red) & along pattern's right angle edge.

3. Fold seam allowance to the wrong side and press. Repeat for all triangles from step 2.

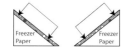

Fold & press seam allowance over pattern angle edge.

4. Place fabric triangles, two of each variation, on one 8½" x 12½" Fabric A piece. Refer to Hand Appliqué on page 109 to stitch angled edges in place.

Hand or machine appliqué triangles

5. Repeat steps 1-4 to make two additional units, one of each fabric combination.

6. Refer to Quick Fuse Appliqué on page 109. Use pattern on page 86 to trace three owls on paper side of fusible web. Use appropriate fabrics to prepare all appliqués for fusing.

7. Refer to photo on page 83 and layout to position and fuse appliqués to units from steps 4 and 5. Finish appliqué edges with machine satin stitch or other decorative stitching as desired. Owl Block measures 8½" x 12½".

Making the Large Pinwheels Blocks

1. Draw a diagonal line on wrong side of one 5" Fabric C square. Place marked square and one 5" Fabric D square right sides together. Sew scant ¼" away from drawn line on both sides to make half-square triangles as shown. Make two. Cut on drawn line and press. Square to 4½". This will make four half-square triangle units.

Fabric C = 5 x 5   Square to 4½"
Fabric D = 5 x 5   Make 4
Make 2   Half-Square Triangle Units

2. Sew two units from step 1 together as shown. Press. Make two. Sew these two units together as shown. Refer to Twisting Seams on page 108 and press. Large Pinwheel Block measures 8½" square.

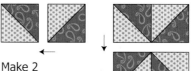

Make 2

Block measures 8½"

3. Repeat steps 1 and 2 to make two additional blocks using different fabric combinations.

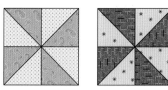

Making the Small Pinwheels Blocks

1. Draw a diagonal line on wrong side of one 3" Fabric E square. Place marked square and one 3" Fabric F square right sides together. Sew scant ¼" away from drawn line on both sides to make half-square triangles as shown. Make four. Cut on drawn line and press. Square to 2½". This will make eight half-square triangle units.

Fabric E = 3 x 3   Square to 2½"
Fabric F = 3 x 3   Make 8
Make 4   Half-Square Triangle Units

2. Sew two units from step 1 together as shown. Press. Make four. Sew two of these units together as shown. Refer to Twisting Seams on page 108 and press. Make two. Small Pinwheel Block measures 4½" square.

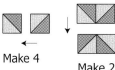

Make 4

Make 2
Block meausres 4½"

3. Repeat steps 1 and 2 to make four additional blocks, two of each fabric combination.

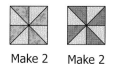

Make 2   Make 2

Assembling the Quilt

This quilt will be constructed by sewing vertical rows instead of our normal horizontal row construction.

1. Referring to photo on page 83 and layout on page 84, arrange all blocks in rows. Sew two Small Pinwheel Blocks together. Refer to Twisting Seams on page 108 and press. Make three.

Make 3

2. Sew one unit from step 1 between one Owl Block and one Large Pinwheel Block. Press seams toward Owl Block and Large Pinwheel Block.

3. Sew one unit from step 1 between one Large Pinwheel Block and one Owl Block. Press seams toward Owl Block and Large Pinwheel Block.

4. Sew one Owl Block between one unit from step 1 and one Large Pinwheel Block. Press seams toward Owl Block.

5. Sew rows together. Press.

6. Sew 1" x 24½" First Border strips to top and bottom of quilt. Press seams toward border. Sew 1" x 25½" First Border strips to sides. Press.

7. Refer to photo on page 83 and layout on page 84 noting Outside Border orientation. Sew 25½" x 2" Outside Border strip to top of quilt. Press seams toward border

8. Sew 27" x 2" Outside Border strip to right side of quilt. Press. Sew 27" x 2" Outside Border strip to bottom of quilt. Press.

9. Sew 28½" x 2" Outside Border strip to left side of quilt. Press.

Finishing the Quilt

1. Referring to Layering the Quilt on page 110, arrange and baste backing, batting, and top together. Hand or machine quilt as desired.

2. Refer to Binding the Quilt on page 110. Use 2¼"-wide Binding strips to bind quilt. Note: Finished width of binding is ¼" instead of our normal ½".

Flights of Fancy
Wall Quilt Pattern

Tracing Line_____

Tracing Line ....
(will be hidden behind other fabrics)

Stitching Line – – – – – – –

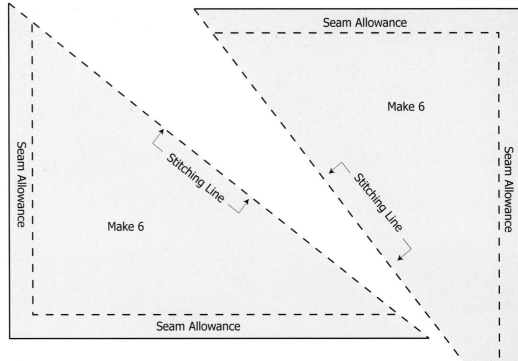

Seam Allowance

Seam Allowance

Make 6

Stitching Line

Stitching Line

Seam Allowance

Make 6

Seam Allowance

Seam Allowance

Our owls have personality plus by simply changing the eyes, wings, and feet placement. Refer to photo on page 83 prior to fusing appliqués.

Wise Old Owl Pincushion

This wise old pincushion is just what you need to add some fun to the sewing room. Felted wool and embroidered accents make this fellow as handsome as he is useful.

Preparing the Appliqués

1. Refer to Quick Fuse Appliqué on page 109. Use patterns below to trace owl's head, beak, wings, and feet on paper side of fusible web. Use appropriate fabrics to prepare all appliqués for fusing.

2. Note: Appliqués extend past the pincushion base. The two layers will add body and durability to the appliqués. Fuse head, wings, and feet appliqués to wool fabric scraps. Cut bottom fabric to match top appliqué piece.

3. Fuse beak to head.

Making the Pincushion

1. Refer to Circle Template on page 111. Trace 5" circle on template plastic or pattern paper. Cut out circle on drawn line.

2. Trace circle template on two 6" Pincushion squares. Cut out circle on drawn line.

3. Using a ¼"-wide seam, sew 2¾" x 13" Gusset piece short sides together to form a loop. Press.

4. Referring to photo for feet placement, place feet on top circle aligning straight edge with circle edge. (Feet should be pointing in toward center). Using ½"-wide seam, sew top circle to gusset. Sew bottom circle to unit leaving a 3" opening for turning.

5. Turn unit inside out and fill Pincushion with polyester fiberfill. Add beanbag pellets to bottom area to add weight to piece. Hand-stitch opening closed.

6. Referring to photo, arrange owl elements on pincushion.

7. Referring to Embroidery Guide on page 111 and using a blanket stitch and three strands of embroidery floss, sew owl elements to pincushion stitching securely to base and finishing edges on overhanging areas. Using a stem stitch and three strands of embroidery floss, stitch feather accents to owl chest. Sew on buttons for eyes.

SUPPLIES

Pincushion Top & Bottom - Wool scraps
Two 6" squares

Gusset - Wool scrap
One 2¾" x 13"

Appliqué - Assorted wool scraps

Heavyweight Fusible Web - Scrap

Embroidery Floss

Polyester Fiberfill

Bean Bag Pellets

Assorted Buttons - 4

**Wise Old Owl
Pincushion Pattern**
Tracing Line _____
Tracing Line --------------------
(will be hidden behind other fabrics)
Placement Line --·--·--·--·--
Embroidery Placement ············

Beautiful Birds
Wall Quilt

Stylized birds observe the world from their perches on a beautifully blended batik wall quilt. Soft colors, simple shapes, and charming details make this quilt a sweet spot of serenity in a busy world.

Beautiful Birds Wall Quilt Finished Size: 35¼" x 35¼"	FIRST CUT		SECOND CUT	
	Number of Strips or Pieces	Dimensions	Number of Pieces	Dimensions
Fabric A Background ⅝ yard	1	5½" x 42"	6	5½" squares* *cut twice diagonally
			2	3" squares** **cut once diagonally
	7	1½" x42"	6	1½" x 20"
Fabric B Appliqué Background ⅓ yard	1	9½" x 42"	4	9½" squares
Fabric C Appliqué Block Accent ¼ yard	2	3½" x 42"	16	3½" squares
Fabric D Accent Squares ¼ yard	2	3½" x 42"	16	3½" squares
Fabric E Nine-Patch (Purple) ⅛ yard each of 2 Fabrics	1***	1½" x 42" ***cut for each fabric		
Fabric F Nine-Patch (Green) ⅛ yard each of 3 Fabrics	1***	1½" x 42" ***cut for each fabric	2***	1½" x 20"
Fabric G Nine-Patch (Blue) ⅛ yard each of 3 Fabrics	1***	1½" x 42" ***cut for each fabric	2***	1½" x 20"
First Border ⅙ yard	4	1" x 42"	2	1" x 31¼"
			2	1" x 30¼"
Outside Border ⅓ yard	4	2¼" x 42"	2	2¼" x 34¾"
			2	2¼" x 31¼"
Binding ⅜ yard	4	2¾" x 42"		

Backing - 1⅛ yards
Batting - 40" x 40"
Appliqué - Assorted scraps

Lightweight Fusible Web - ⅝ yard
Assorted Beads
Embroidery Floss

Fabric Requirements and Cutting Instructions

Read all instructions before beginning and use ¼"-wide seam allowances throughout. Read Cutting Strips and Pieces on page 108 prior to cutting fabric.

Getting Started

This must-have quilt will bring a smile to your face with its fresh color palette, interesting block setting, and whimsical birds. Nine-Patch Block measures 3½" square (unfinished) and Bird Block measures 9½" (unfinished). Refer to Accurate Seam Allowance on page 108. Whenever possible use Assembly Line Method on page 108. Press seams in direction of arrows.

Making the Bird Block

Refer to appliqué instructions on page 109. Our instructions are for Quick-Fuse Appliqué, but if you prefer hand appliqué, reverse patterns and add ¼"-wide seam allowances.

TIP

Artistic Expression

Create the unexpected by using a simple embroidery stitch and embroidery floss to add detail, depth, and texture to each large flower. Sewing a few beads to the quilt for bird eyes and flower details will add sparkle to your quilt.

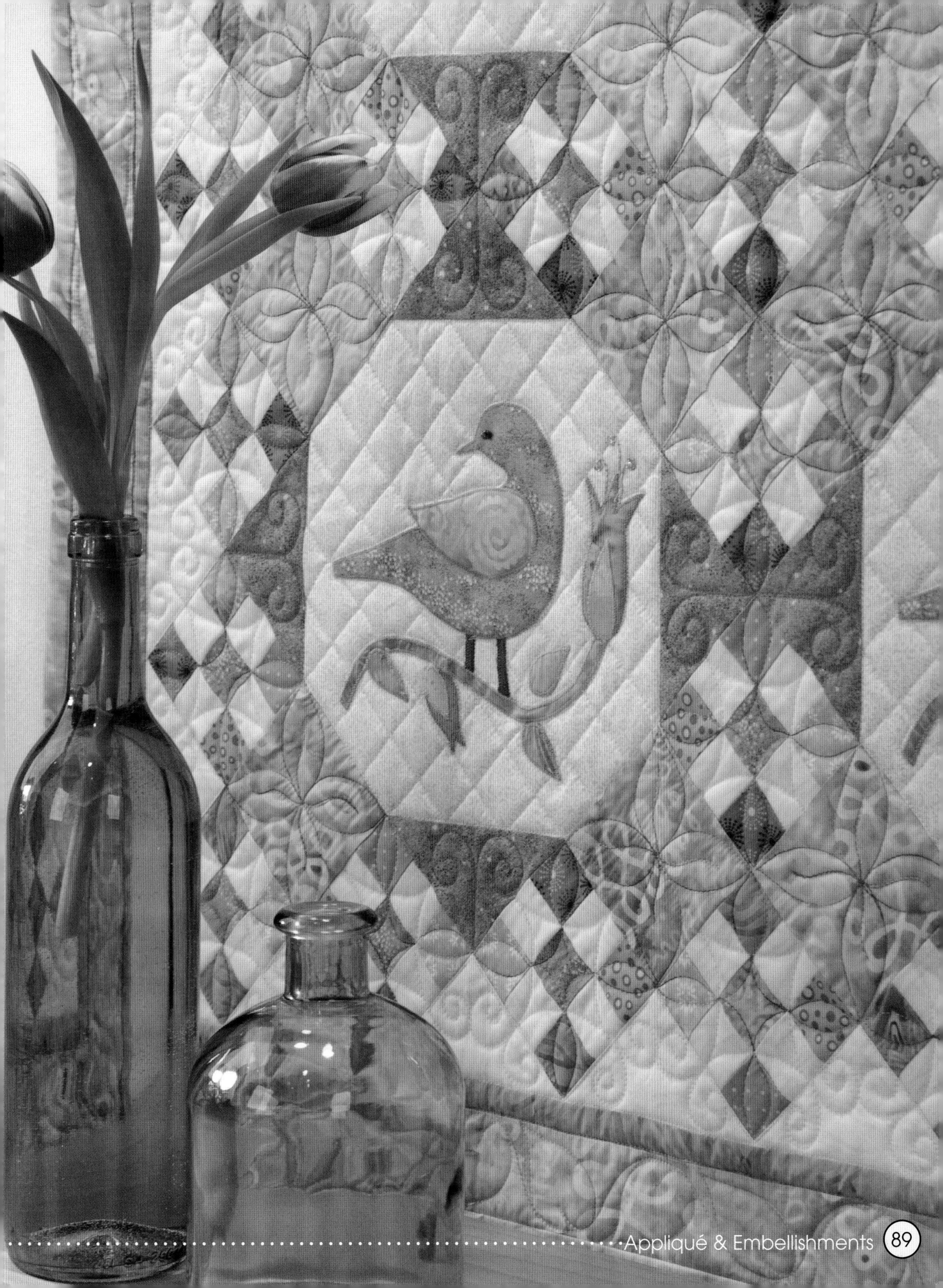

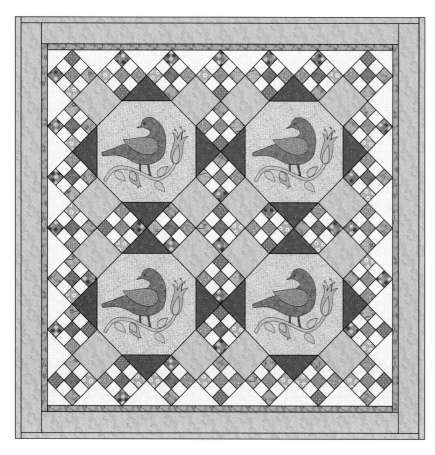

Beautiful Birds Wall Quilt
35¼" x 35¼"

1. Refer to Quick Corner Triangles on page 108. Making quick corner triangle units, sew four 3½" Fabric C squares to one 9½" Fabric B square. Press. Make four.

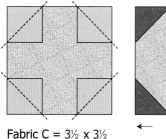

Fabric C = 3½ x 3½
Fabric B = 9½ x 9½
Make 4

2. Use patterns on page 93 to trace bird, flowers, branch, and leaves on paper side of fusible web. Use appropriate fabrics to prepare all appliqués for fusing.

3. Refer to photo on page 89 and layout. Note: Blocks are set on-point. Position and fuse appliqués to block accordingly. Finish appliqué edges with machine satin stitch or other decorative stitching as desired. Make four. Block measures 9½" square.

Making the Nine-Patch Blocks

1. Sew one 1½" x 42" Fabric E strip between two 1½" x 42" Fabric A strips as shown to make a strip set. Press seams toward Fabric A. Make two, one of each combination. Cut strip set into thirty-three 1½"-wide segments as shown.

1½

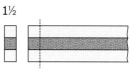

Make 2
(one of each combination)
Cut 33 segments

2. Sew one 1½" x 20" Fabric A strip between one 1½" x 20" Fabric G strip and one 1½" x 20" Fabric F strip as shown to make a strip set. Press seams toward Fabric A. Make a total of six strip sets using different Fabric F and G combinations. Cut strip set into sixty-six 1½"-wide segments as shown.

1½

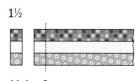

Make 6
Cut 66 segments

3. Sew one unit from step 1 between two units from step 2 as shown. Press. Note: Four Corner Blocks are made with the blue accents on one side and green accents on the other. Make twenty-nine Nine-Patch Blocks alternating green and blue accent placements. Block measures 3½" square.

Corner Block   **Nine-Patch Block**

Make 4   Make 29
Block measures 3½"   (in assorted combinations)
                         Block measures 3½"

Assembling the Quilt

1. Sew one small Fabric A triangle to one Corner Block as shown. Triangle ends will extend past block edges. Press. Sew this unit between two large Fabric A triangles as shown. Press. Make four.

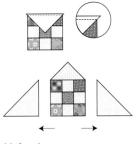

Make 4

2. Sew one 3½" Fabric D square between two Nine-Patch blocks as shown. Press. Make ten. Sew one unit from step 1 to one unit from this step. Press. Make four and label Unit 1.

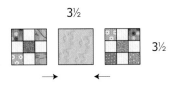

Make 10

Unit 1

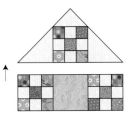

Make 4

3. Sew two Fabric A large triangles to one Nine-Patch block as shown. Press. Make four.

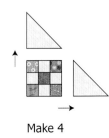

Make 4

4. Sew one Nine-Patch block between one 3½" Fabric D square and one large Fabric A triangle as shown. Press. Make four.

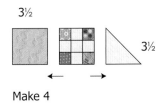

Make 4

5. Sew one unit from step 2 to one large Fabric A triangle as shown. Press. Make four.

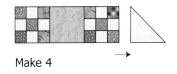

Make 4

6. Sew one unit from step 4 between one unit each from steps 3 and 5 as shown. Press. Make four and label Unit 2.

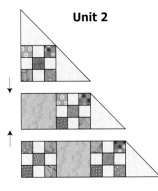

Unit 2

Make 4

7. Sew one Nine-Patch block between two 3½" Fabric D squares as shown. Press.

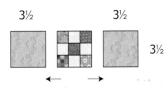

8. Sew unit from step 7 between two units from step 2 as shown. Press and label Unit 3.

Unit 3

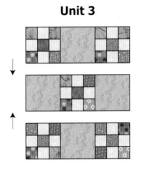

9. Refer to photo on page 89 and layout on page 90 to check Bird Block orientation prior to sewing. Sew one Unit 1 to one Bird Block as shown. Press. Make two, as shown.

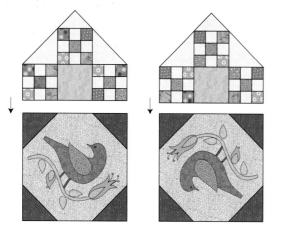

10. Sew one unit from step 9 between two of Unit 2, checking orientation of units prior to sewing. Press. Make two.

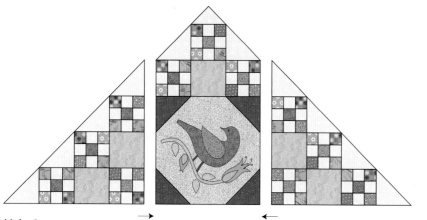

Make 2

11. Refer to photo on page 89 and diagram below to check Bird Block orientation prior to sewing. Sew together two of Unit 1, two Bird Blocks, and one Unit 3. Press.

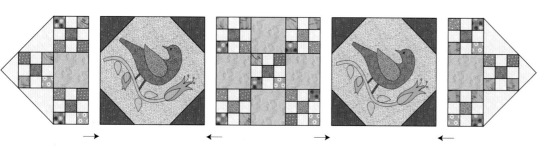

12. Referring to photo on page 89 and layout on page 90, sew unit from step 11 between units from step 10. Press.

Adding the Borders

1. Sew two 1" x 30¼" First Border strips to top and bottom of quilt. Press seams toward border. Sew two 1" x 31¼" First Border strips to sides. Press.

2. Sew two 2¼" x 31¼" Outside Border strips to top and bottom of quilt. Press seams toward border just added. Sew two 2¼" x 34¾" Outside Border strips to sides. Press.

Finishing the Quilt

1. Referring to Layering the Quilt on page 110, arrange and baste backing, batting, and top together. Hand or machine quilt as desired.

2. Refer to photo on page 89, appliqué pattern on page 93, and Embroidery Stitch guide on page 111. Using a stem stitch and two strands of embroidery floss, embroider flower detail. Sew beads to flowers. Use beads or French Knots for birds' eyes.

3. Refer to Binding the Quilt on page 110. Use 2¾"-wide binding strips to bind quilt.

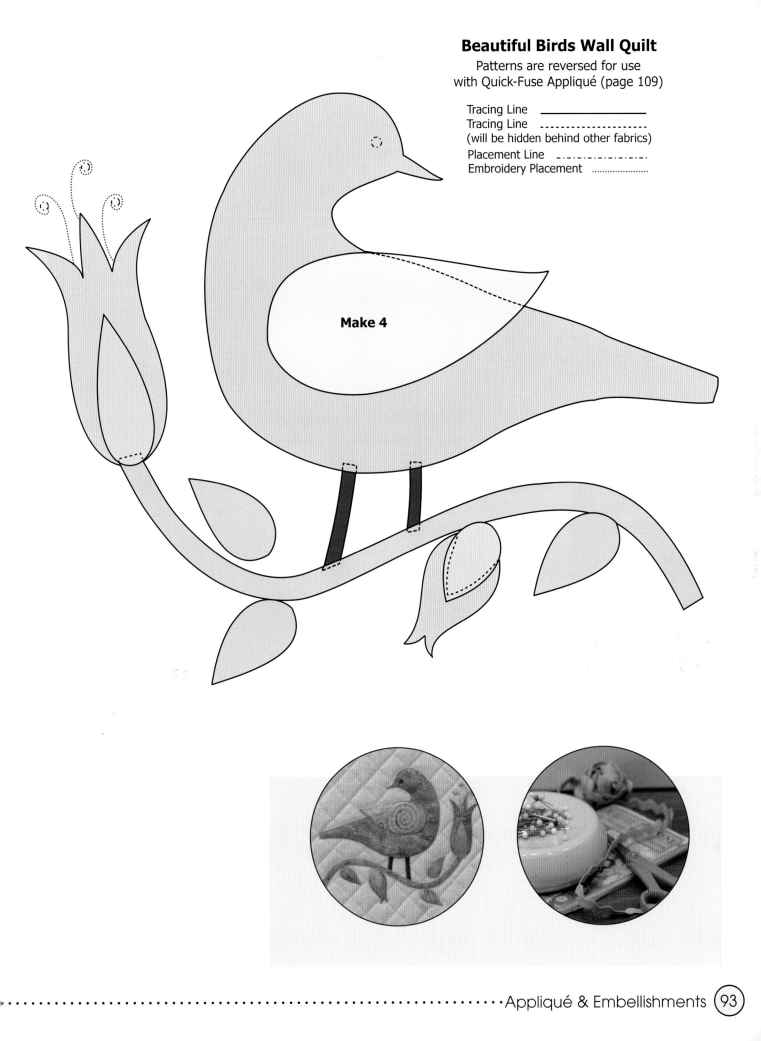

Beautiful Birds Wall Quilt

Patterns are reversed for use
with Quick-Fuse Appliqué (page 109)

Tracing Line ————————
Tracing Line - - - - - - - - - - - -
(will be hidden behind other fabrics)
Placement Line - · - · - · - · - · -
Embroidery Placement · · · · · · · · · ·

Make 4

Framed Flowers
Wall Quilt

Couched stems, embroidered accents, and quilting details make this appliquéd art piece perfect for fabric framing. A series of borders creates a frame for this appliquéd bouquet.

Framed Flowers Wall Quilt Finished Size: 23" x 27"	FIRST CUT		SECOND CUT	
	Number of Strips or Pieces	Dimensions	Number of Pieces	Dimensions
Fabric A Background ½ yard	1	12½" x 42"	1	12½" x 16½"
Fabric B Accent Squares ⅛ yard	1	1½" x 42"	20	1½" squares
First Border ⅛ yard	2	1" x 42"	2	1" x 16½"
			2	1" x 12½"
Second Border ¼ yard	2	1½" x 42"	2	1½" x 18½"
			2	1½" x 14½"
	2	1" x 42"	2	1" x 16½"
			2	1" x 12½"
Third Border ¼ yard	3	1½" x 42"	2	1½" x 20½"
			2	1½" x 16½"
Fourth Border ¼ yard	3	1½" x 42"	2	1½" x 22½"
			2	1½" x 18½"
Outside Border ¼ yard	4	1½" x 42"	2	1½" x 24½"
			2	1½" x 20½"
Binding ⅜ yard	4	2¾" x 42"		

Appliqué Vase - 8" square scrap
Appliqués - Assorted scraps
Backing - ¾ yard
Batting - 27" x 31"
Lightweight Fusible Web - ⅝ yard
Yarn
Embroidery Floss

Fabric Requirements and Cutting Instructions

Read all instructions before beginning and use ¼"-wide seam allowances throughout. Read Cutting Strips and Pieces on page 108 prior to cutting fabric.

Getting Started

Gradated shades of colored borders accent this bouquet of flowers. Refer to Accurate Seam Allowance on page 108. Press seams in direction of arrows.

Making the Quilt

Press all seams toward border just sewn unless otherwise stated.

1. Sew 1" x 12½" First Border strip to one 1" x 12½" Second Border strip. Press seams toward Second Border. Make two.

Make 2

Artistic Expression

TIP

Add the unexpected to a quilt by adding texture through the use of yarn or other fibers. To couch yarn/fiber to quilt, use a zigzag stitch a little wider than fiber. It is very important that the yarn/fiber has the same laundry needs as fabric. To test colorfastness, place a small yarn/fiber piece in a glass of hot water. If the water changes color don't use this fiber.

Framed Flowers Wall Quilt
23" x 27"

2. Sew 12½" x 16½" Fabric A piece between two units from step 1 as shown. Press.

12½

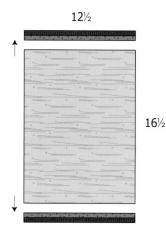

16½

3. Sew 1" x 16½" First Border strip to one 1" x 16½" Second Border strip. Press seams toward Second Border. Make two.

4. Sew one unit from step 3 between two 1½" Fabric B squares as shown. Press. Make two. Sew to sides of unit from step 2. Press.

Make 2

5. Refer to photo on page 95 and layout for all remaining steps. Sew two 1½" x 14½" Second Border strips to top and bottom of quilt unit from step 4. Press. Sew one 1½" x 18½" Second Border strip between two 1½" Fabric B squares. Press seams toward Second Border. Make two. Sew border unit to sides of quilt unit. Press.

6. Sew two 1½" x 16½" Third Border strips to top and bottom of quilt unit. Press. Sew one 1½" x 20½" Third Border strip between two 1½" Fabric B squares. Press. Make two. Sew border unit to sides of quilt unit. Press.

7. Sew two 1½" x 18½" Fourth Border strips to top and bottom of quilt unit. Press. Sew one 1½" x 22½" Fourth Border strip between two 1½" Fabric B squares. Press. Make two. Sew border unit to sides of quilt unit. Press.

8. Sew two 1½" x 20½" Outside Border strips to top and bottom of quilt unit. Press. Sew one 1½" x 24½" Outside Border strip between two 1½" Fabric B squares. Press. Make two. Sew border unit to sides of quilt unit. Press.

Adding the Appliqués

Refer to appliqué instructions on page 109. Our instructions are for Quick-Fuse Appliqué, but if you prefer hand appliqué, reverse patterns and add ¼"-wide seam allowances.

1. Use patterns on pages 97-99 to trace vase, flowers, and leaves on paper side of fusible web. Use appropriate fabrics to prepare all appliqués for fusing.

2. Refer to photo on page 95 and layout to arrange vase, yarn and flowers on quilt. Pin stems in place. Yarn will go over vase inside piece and extend under vase lip. Remove vase base and lip, and flowers. Fuse vase inside piece to quilt, carefully lift yarn from vase piece prior to fusing, then reposition yarn.

3. Using a zigzag stitch a little wider than yarn and normal stitch length, stitch yarn to quilt.

4. Refer to photo on page 95 and layout to position and fuse vase base and lip, flowers, and leaves to quilt. Finish appliqué edges with machine satin stitch or other decorative stitching as desired.

5. Refer to photo on page 95, layout, and appliqué patterns on pages 97-99 for embroidery stitch lines. Using a fabric removable marker, trace embroidery lines to quilt.

6. Refer to Embroidery stitch guide on page 111 for stem stitch. Using three strands of floss, stitch flower details to quilt.

Finishing the Quilt

1. Referring to Layering the Quilt on page 110, arrange and baste backing, batting, and top together. Hand or machine quilt as desired.

2. Refer to Binding the Quilt on page 110. Use 2¾"-wide Binding strips to bind quilt.

Framed Flowers Wall Quilt

Tracing Line ——————————

Tracing Line ------------------
(will be hidden behind other fabrics)

Embroidery Placement ··················

Embroidery Placement ··················
(will be hidden by fabrics)

Placement Line –·–·–·–·–·–·–

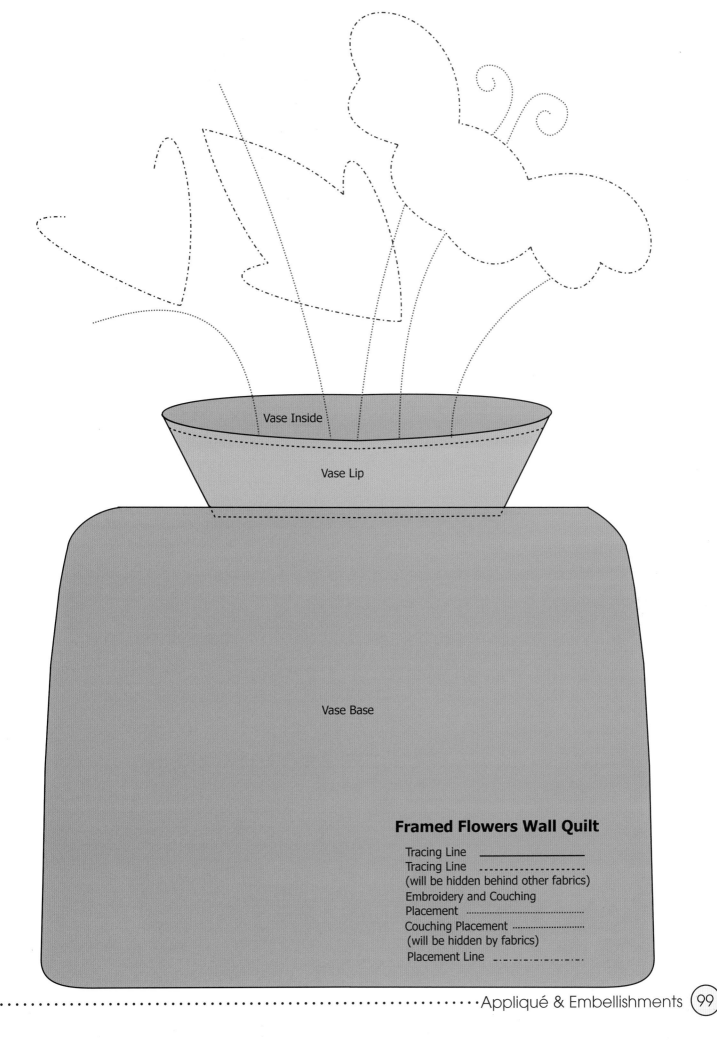

Vase Inside

Vase Lip

Vase Base

Framed Flowers Wall Quilt

Tracing Line ————————

Tracing Line ·····················
(will be hidden behind other fabrics)

Embroidery and Couching
Placement ·····················

Couching Placement ·····················
(will be hidden by fabrics)

Placement Line ·····················

Tulip Medallion
Lap Quilt

Striking colors, complex-looking piecing, and beautiful appliqué combine to create this stunning medallion-style quilt. An appliquéd border adds a traditional touch to this handsome heirloom.

Tulip Medallion Lap Quilt Finished Size: 52½" x 52½"	FIRST CUT		SECOND CUT	
	Number of Strips or Pieces	Dimensions	Number of Pieces	Dimensions
Fabric A Background & Pieced Border ⅞ yard	1	18" x 42"	1	18" square
	3	2½" x 42"	1	2½" x 13"
			4	2½" squares
Fabric B First Accent Border & Corner Star Accents ½ yard	1	7½" x 42"	2	7½" squares
	1	4" x 42"	8	4" squares
	2	1¼" x 42"	2	1¼" x 19½"
			2	1¼" x 18"
Fabric C Second Accent Border & Corner Star Center Accent ⅜ yard	1	6½" x 42"	4	6½" squares
	3	1½" x 42"	2	1½" x 21½"
			2	1½" x 19½"
Fabric D Third Accent Border & Corner Star Background ⅞ yard	1	7½" x 42"	2	7½" squares
	1	4" x 42"	8	4" squares
	2	3½" x 42"	8	3½" x 6½"
			4	3½" squares
	4	1½" x 42"	2	1½" x 23½"
			2	1½" x 21½"
Fabric E Fourth Accent Border & First Border ½ yard	4	1¾" x 42"	2	1¾" x 26"
			2	1¾" x 23½"
	4	1½" x 42"	2	1½" x 38½"
			2	1½" x 36½"
Fabric F Corner Triangle Accent (Gold) ¼ yard	2	3½" x 42"	12	3½" squares
Fabric G Corner Triangle Accent (Green) ⅓ yard	1	7½" x 42"	4	7½" squares
Fabric H Corner Triangle (Red) ¼ yard	2	3½" x 42"	12	3½" squares

Tulip Medallion Lap Quilt CONTINUED	FIRST CUT		SECOND CUT	
	Number of Strips or Pieces	Dimensions	Number of Pieces	Dimensions
Fabric I Pieced Border ⅓ yard	3	2½" x 42"	2	2½" x 13"
Fabric J Appliqué Border Background ¾ yard	5	4½" x 42"		
Outside Border ⅓ yard	6	1¼" x 42"		
Binding ⅝ yard	6	2¾" x 42"		

Vine Appliqué - ⅔ yard
Flower Appliqués - Assorted scraps
Leaf Appliqués - Assorted scraps
Backing - 3¼ yards
Batting - 58" x 58"
Lightweight Fusible Web - 1½ yards
Bias Tape Maker Tool

Fabric Requirements and Cutting Instructions

Read all instructions before beginning and use ¼"-wide seam allowances throughout. Read Cutting Strips and Pieces on page 108 prior to cutting fabric.

Getting Started

Various shades of colored borders accent this bouquet of flowers. Refer to Accurate Seam Allowance on page 108. Press seams in direction of arrows.

Making the Center Block

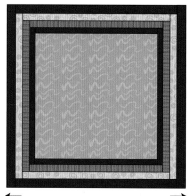

TIP

Artistic Expressions

Don't be afraid to combine techniques in a quilt. The pieced blocks in this quilt add structure, while the appliqués add movement and grace. The unique pieced triangle units give the appearance of whole blocks running under the center block.

Tulip Medallion Lap Quilt
52½" x 52½"

1. Refer to diagram on page 100 for all Center Block steps. Sew 18" Fabric A square between two 1¼" x 18" Fabric B strips. Press seams toward border. Sew this unit between two 1¼" x 19½" Fabric B strips. Press.

2. Sew unit from step 1 between two 1½" x 19½" Fabric C strips. Press seams toward border. Sew this unit between two 1½" x 21½" Fabric C strips. Press.

3. Sew unit from step 2 between two 1½" x 21½" Fabric D strips. Press seams toward border. Sew this unit between two 1½" x 23½" Fabric D strips. Press.

4. Sew unit from step 1 between two 1¾" x 23½" Fabric E strips. Press seams toward border. Sew this unit between two 1¾" x 26" Fabric E strips. Press.

Adding the Appliqués

Refer to appliqué instructions on page 109. Our instructions are for Quick-Fuse Appliqué, but if you prefer hand appliqué, reverse patterns and add ¼"-wide seam allowances.

1. Use patterns on pages 106 and 107 to trace Center Tulip flowers, stems, and leaves on paper side of fusible web. Use appropriate fabrics to prepare all appliqués for fusing.

2. Refer to photo on page 101 and layout to position and fuse appliqués to quilt. Finish appliqué edges with machine satin stitch or other decorative stitching as desired.

Making the Corner Star Blocks

1. Draw a diagonal line on wrong side of one 4" Fabric D square. Place marked square and one 4" Fabric B square right sides together. Sew scant ¼" away from drawn line on both sides to make half-square triangles as shown. Make eight. Cut on drawn line and press. Square to 3½". This will make sixteen half-square triangle units.

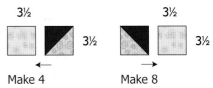

Fabric D = 4 x 4   Square to 3½"
Fabric I = 4 x 4   Make 16
Make 8   Half-Square Triangle Units

2. Sew one 3½" Fabric F square to one unit from step 1 as shown. Press. Make twelve, four of one combination and eight of the other.

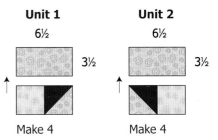

Make 4   Make 8

3. Sew one 3½" x 6½" Fabric D piece to unit from step 2 as shown. Press. Make eight, four of each variation. Label Unit 1 and Unit 2 as shown.

Unit 1   **Unit 2**
6½   6½

Make 4   Make 4

4. Sew one unit from step 1 to one 3½" Fabric D square as shown. Press. Sew this unit to one unit from step 2. Press. Make four and label Unit 3.

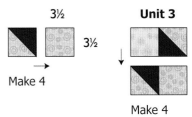

Make 4   Make 4

5. Refer to Quick Corner Triangles on page 108. Making quick corner triangle units, sew three 3½" Fabric H squares to one 6½" Fabric C square as shown. Press. Make four and label Unit 4.

Unit 4

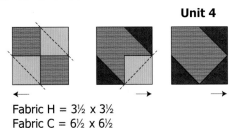

Fabric H = 3½ x 3½
Fabric C = 6½ x 6½
Make 4

6. Making half-square triangles (refer to step 1), sew one 7½" Fabric D square to one 7½" Fabric G square as shown. Press. Make two. This makes four half-square triangle units.

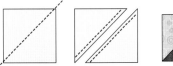

Fabric D = 7½ x 7½
Fabric G = 7½ x 7½
Make 2

Make 4
Half-Square Triangle Units

7. Making half-square triangles, sew one 7½" Fabric G square to one 7½" Fabric B square as shown. Press. Make two. This makes four half-square triangle units.

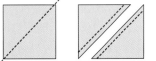

Fabric G = 7½ x 7½
Fabric B = 7½ x 7½
Make 2

Make 4
Half-Square Triangle Units

8. Draw a diagonal line on wrong side of one unit from step 6. Place marked piece and one unit from step 7 right sides together positioning Fabric G sections on Fabric D and Fabric B. Sew a scant ¼" away from drawn line on both sides as shown. Make four. Cut on drawn line. Refer to Twisting Seams on page 108 and press. Square unit to 6½" and label Unit 5. This will make eight quarter-square triangle units.

Unit 5

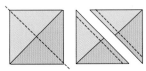

Unit from step 6
Unit from step 7
Make 4

Square to 6½"
Make 8
Quarter-Square Triangle Units

9. Sew one Unit 5 between one Unit 1 and one Unit 3 as shown. Press. Make four. Sew one Unit 4 to one Unit 5 as shown. Press. Make four.

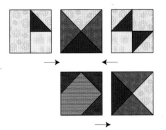

10. Referring to diagram, arrange and sew one of each unit from step 9 and one Unit 2 as shown. Press. Make four.

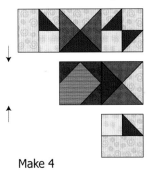

Make 4

11. Align one triangle unit from step 10 with Center Block right sides together as shown. Sew using ¼"-wide seam allowance. Note: Stitch line will line up with unit tips. Trim along Center Block edge to remove excess block pieces. Press. Repeat to sew remaining triangles to block.

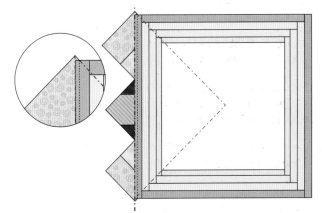

12. Sew two 1½" x 36½" Fabric E strips to top and bottom of unit from step 11. Press seams toward border. Sew two 1½" x 38½" Fabric E strips to sides of unit. Press.

13. Sew together lengthwise two 2½" x 42" Fabric A strips and two 2½" x 42" Fabric I strips to make a strip set alternating fabric placement. Press toward Fabric I. Cut strip set into sixteen 2½"-wide segments as shown.

2½

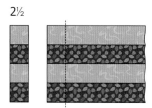

Cut 16 segments

14. Sew together lengthwise two 2½" x 13" Fabric I strips and one 2½" x 13" Fabric A strip alternating fabric placement. Press. Cut strip set into four 2½"-wide segments as shown.

2½

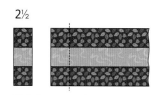

Cut 4 segments

15. Arrange and sew together four units from step 13 and one unit from step 14. Press. Make four.

Make 4

16. Sew two strips from step 15 to top and bottom of quilt. Press seams toward center unit.

17. Sew unit from step 15 between two 2½" Fabric A squares. Press. Make two. Sew to sides of quilt. Press.

2½   2½

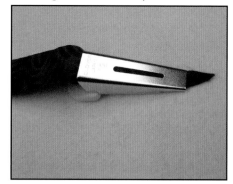

2½

Make 2

18. Refer to Adding the Borders on page 110. Sew 4½" x 42" Fabric J strips together end-to-end to make one continuous 4½"-wide Fabric J strip. Measure quilt through center from side to side. Cut two 4½"-wide Fabric J strips to this measurement. Sew to top and bottom of quilt. Press seams toward border.

19. Measure quilt through center from top to bottom including border just added. Cut two 4½"-wide Fabric J strips to this measurement. Sew to sides of quilt. Press.

20. Refer to steps 18 and 19 to join, measure, trim and sew 1¼"-wide Outside Border strips to top, bottom, and sides of quilt. Press.

Making the Bias Vine

1. Cut one 24" Vine Appliqué fabric square. Refer to Making Bias Strips page 110 to make 1" wide bias strips.

2. Refer to manufacturer's instructions for bias tape maker tool. Cut one end of fabric strip diagonally to form a sharp point as shown.

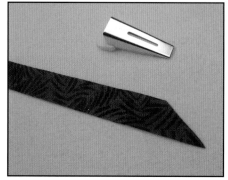

3. Starting at the wide end of the bias tape maker tool, feed point till it comes out of the narrow end. This will automatically fold under the raw edges to create a single fold bias strip.

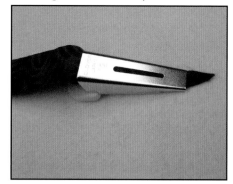

4. Place iron on fabric strip tip while gently pulling tool to the left. Press folded edges as they appear out of the bias tool.

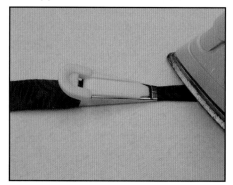

Finishing the Quilt

1. Refer to photo on page 101 and layout on page 102 and bias guide below to position bias stem strip on Fabric F (Applique Border); making sure strip ends will be covered by appliquéd pieces. Hand or machine stitch bias stem to border.

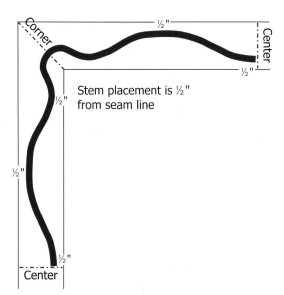

Corner

Center

½"

½"

½"

Stem placement is ½" from seam line

½"

½"

½"

Center

2. Use patterns on page 106 to trace sixteen Tulip Border Flowers and sixteen Tulip Border Leaves on paper side of fusible web. Use appropriate fabrics to prepare all appliqués for fusing.

3. Refer to photo on page 101 and layout on page 102 to position and fuse appliqués to quilt border. Finish appliqué edges with machine satin stitch or other decorative stitching as desired

4. Cut backing crosswise into two equal pieces. Sew pieces together lengthwise to make one 58" x 80" (approximate) backing piece. Press and trim to 58" x 58".

5. Referring to Layering the Quilt on page 110, arrange and baste backing, batting, and top together. Hand or machine quilt as desired.

6. Refer to Binding the Quilt on page 110. Sew 2¾" x 42" binding strips end-to-end to make one continuous 2¾"-wide binding strip. Bind quilt to finish.

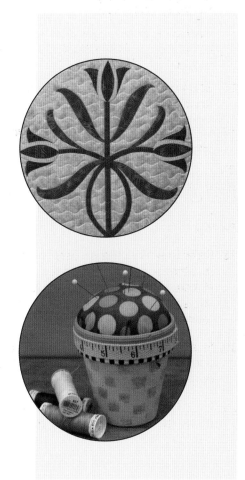

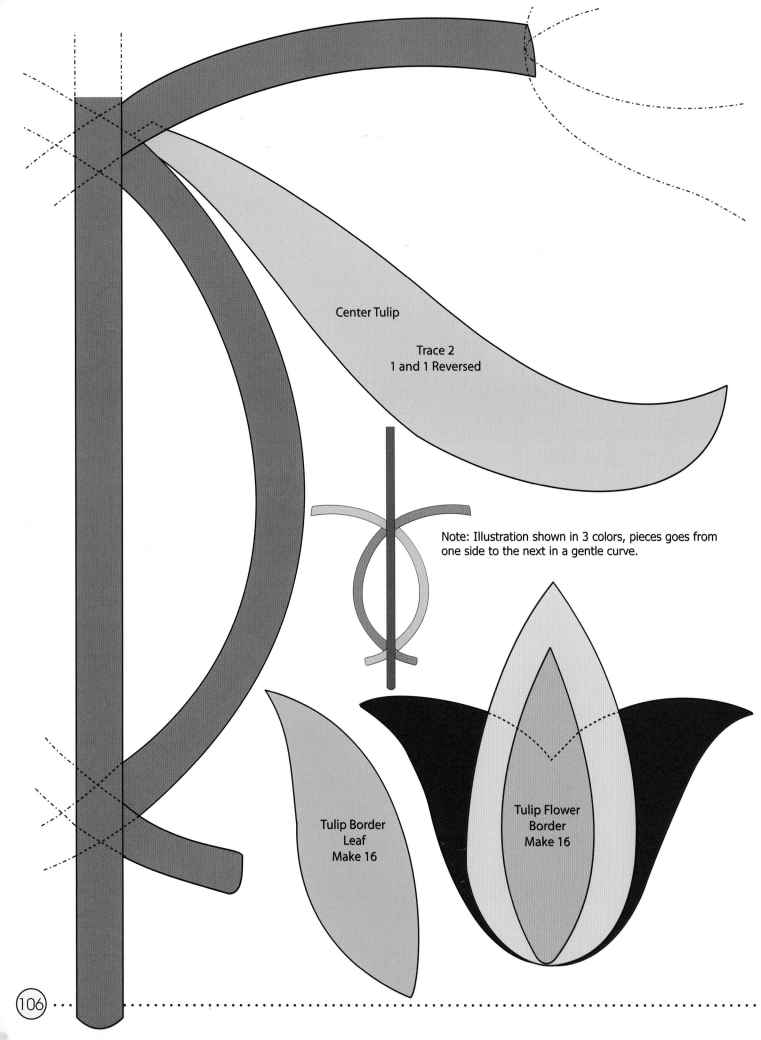

Center Tulip

Trace 2
1 and 1 Reversed

Note: Illustration shown in 3 colors, pieces goes from one side to the next in a gentle curve.

Tulip Border
Leaf
Make 16

Tulip Flower
Border
Make 16

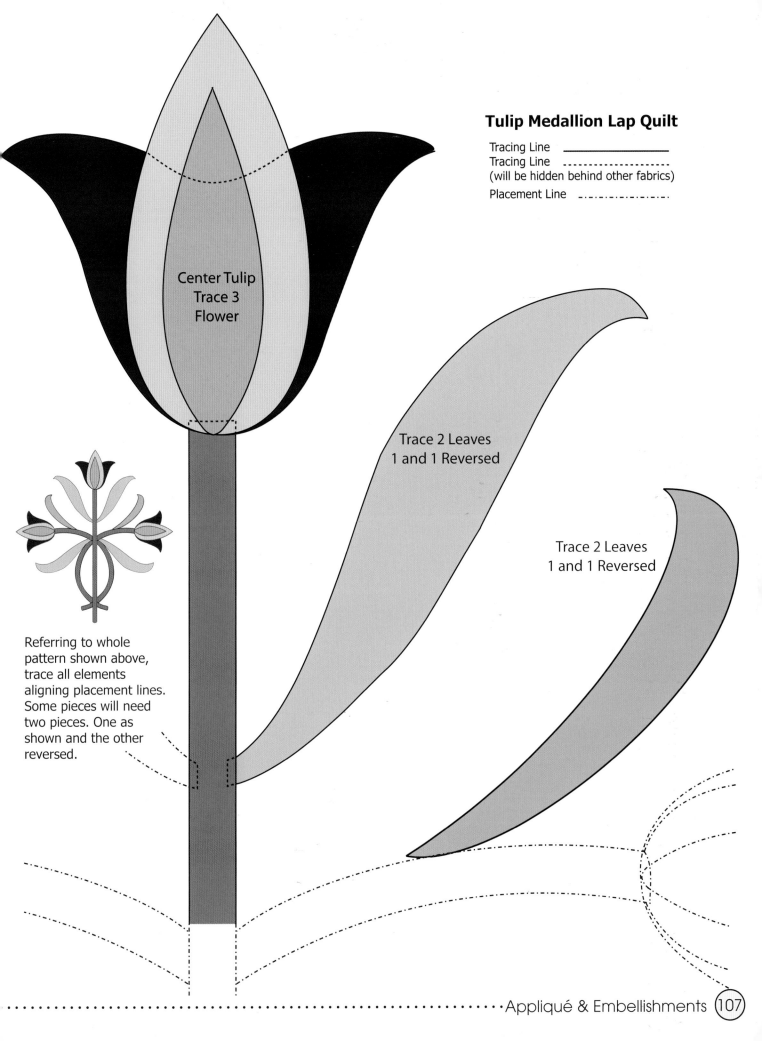

Tulip Medallion Lap Quilt

Tracing Line _____

Tracing Line - - - - - - - - - - - - - -
(will be hidden behind other fabrics)

Placement Line - - - - - - - - - - - -

Center Tulip
Trace 3
Flower

Trace 2 Leaves
1 and 1 Reversed

Trace 2 Leaves
1 and 1 Reversed

Referring to whole
pattern shown above,
trace all elements
aligning placement lines.
Some pieces will need
two pieces. One as
shown and the other
reversed.

General DIRECTIONS

Cutting Strips and Pieces

We recommend washing cotton fabrics in cold water and pressing before making projects in this book. Using a rotary cutter, see-through ruler, and a cutting mat, cut the strips and pieces for the project. If indicated on the Cutting Chart, some will need to be cut again into smaller strips and pieces. Make second cuts in order shown to maximize use of fabric. The yardage amounts are based on an approximate fabric width of 42" and Fat Quarters are based on 18" x 22" pieces.

Pressing

Pressing is very important for accurate seam allowances. Press seams using either steam or dry heat with an "up and down" motion. Do not use side-to-side motion as this will distort the unit or block. Set the seam by pressing along the line of stitching, then press seams to one side as indicated by project instructions and diagram arrows.

Twisting Seams

When a block has several seams meeting in the center as shown, there will be less bulk if seam allowances are pressed in a circular type direction and the center intersection "twisted". Remove 1-2 stitches in the seam allowance to enable the center to twist and lay flat. This technique aids in quilt assembly by allowing the seams to fall opposite each other when repeated blocks are next to each other. The technique works well with 4-patch blocks, pinwheel blocks, and quarter-square triangle blocks.

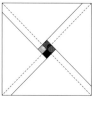

Accurate Seam Allowance

Accurate seam allowances are always important, but especially when the blocks contain many pieces and the quilt top contains multiple pieced borders. If each seam is off as little as ¹⁄₁₆", you'll soon find yourself struggling with components that just won't fit.

To ensure seams are a perfect ¼"-wide, try this simple test: Cut three strips of fabric, each exactly 1½" x 12". With right sides together, and long raw edges aligned, sew two strips together, carefully maintaining a ¼" seam. Press seam to one side. Add the third strip to complete the strip set. Press and measure. The finished strip set should measure 3½" x 12". The center strip should measure 1"-wide, the two outside strips 1¼"-wide, and the seam allowances exactly ¼".

If your measurements differ, check to make sure that seams have been pressed flat. If strip set still doesn't "measure up," try stitching a new strip set, adjusting the seam allowance until a perfect ¼"-wide seam is achieved.

Assembly Line Method

Whenever possible, use an assembly line method. Position pieces right sides together and line up next to sewing machine. Stitch first unit together, then continue sewing others without breaking threads. When all units are sewn, clip threads to separate. Press seams in direction of arrows as shown in step-by-step project diagrams.

Quick Corner Triangles

Quick corner triangles are formed by simply sewing fabric squares to other squares or rectangles. The directions and diagrams with each project illustrate what size pieces to use and where to place squares on the corresponding piece. Follow steps 1–3 below to make quick corner triangle units.

1. With pencil and ruler, draw diagonal line on wrong side of fabric square that will form the triangle. This will be your sewing line.

Sewing line

2. With right sides together, place square on corresponding piece. Matching raw edges, pin in place, and sew ON drawn line. Trim off excess fabric, leaving ¼"-wide seam allowance as shown.

Trim ¼" away from sewing line

3. Press seam in direction of arrow as shown in step-by-step project diagram. Measure completed quick corner triangle unit to ensure the greatest accuracy.

Finished quick corner triangle unit

Fussy Cut

To make a "fussy cut," carefully position ruler or template over a selected design in fabric. Include seam allowances before cutting desired pieces.

Quick-Fuse Appliqué

Quick-fuse appliqué is a method of adhering appliqué pieces to a background with fusible web. For quick and easy results, simply quick-fuse appliqué pieces in place. Use sewable, lightweight fusible web for the projects in this book unless otherwise indicated. Finish raw edges with stitching as desired. Laundering is not recommended unless edges are finished.

1. With paper side up, lay fusible web over appliqué pattern. Leaving ½" space between pieces, trace all elements of design. Cut around traced pieces, approximately ¼" outside traced line.

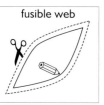

2. With paper side up, position and press fusible web to wrong side of selected fabrics. Follow manufacturer's directions for iron temperature and fusing time. Cut out each piece on traced line.

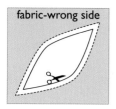

3. Remove paper backing from pieces. A thin film will remain on wrong side of fabric. Position and fuse all pieces of one appliqué design at a time onto background, referring to photos for placement. Fused design will be the reverse of traced pattern.

Appliqué Pressing Sheet

An appliqué pressing sheet is very helpful when there are many small elements to apply using a quick-fuse appliqué technique. The pressing sheet allows small items to be bonded together before applying them to the background. The sheet is coated with a special material that prevents fusible web from adhering permanently to the sheet. Follow manufacturer's directions. Remember to let fabric cool completely before lifting it from the appliqué sheet. If not cooled, the fusible web could remain on the sheet instead of on the fabric.

For accurate layout, place a line drawing of finished project under pressing sheet. Use this as a guide to adhere pieces.

Machine Appliqué

This technique should be used when you are planning to launder quick-fuse projects. Several different stitches can be used: small narrow zigzag stitch, satin stitch, blanket stitch, or another decorative machine stitch. Use an open toe appliqué foot if your machine has one. Use a stabilizer to obtain even stitches and help prevent puckering. Always practice first to check machine settings.

1. Fuse all pieces following Quick-Fuse Appliqué directions.

2. Cut a piece of stabilizer large enough to extend beyond the area to be stitched. Pin to the wrong side of fabric.

3. Select thread to match appliqué.

4. Following the order that appliqués were positioned, stitch along the edges of each section. Anchor beginning and ending stitches by tying off or stitching in place two or three times.

5. Complete all stitching, then remove stabilizer.

Hand Appliqué

Hand appliqué is easy when you start out with the right supplies. Cotton and machine embroidery thread are easy to work with. Pick a color that matches the appliqué fabric as closely as possible. Use appliqué or silk pins for holding shapes in place and a long, thin needle, such as a sharp, for stitching.

1. Make a template for every shape in the appliqué design. Use a dotted line to show where pieces overlap.

2. Place template on right side of appliqué fabric. Trace around template.

3. Cut out shapes ¼" beyond traced line.

4. Position shapes on background fabric, referring to quilt layout. Pin shapes in place.

5. When layering and stitching appliqué shapes, always work from background to foreground. Where shapes overlap, do not turn under and stitch edges of bottom pieces. Turn and stitch the edges of the piece on top.

6. Use the traced line as your turn-under guide. Entering from the wrong side of the appliqué shape, bring the needle up on the traced line. Using the tip of the needle, turn under the fabric along the traced line. Using blind stitch, stitch along folded edge to join the appliqué shape to the background fabric. Turn under and stitch about ¼" at a time.

Adding the Borders

1. Measure quilt through the center from side to side. Trim two border strips to this measurement. Sew to top and bottom of quilt. Press seams toward border.

2. Measure quilt through the center from top to bottom, including borders added in step 1. Trim border strips to this measurement. Sew to sides and press. Repeat to add additional borders.

Layering the Quilt

1. Cut backing and batting 4" to 8" larger than quilt top.

2. Lay pressed backing on bottom (right side down), batting in middle, and pressed quilt top (right side up) on top. Make sure everything is centered and that backing and batting are flat. Backing and batting will extend beyond quilt top.

3. Begin basting in center and work toward outside edges. Baste vertically and horizontally, forming a 3"–4" grid. Baste or pin completely around edge of quilt top. Quilt as desired. Remove basting.

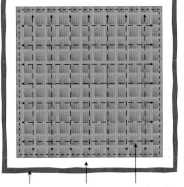

backing   batting   quilt top

Binding the Quilt

1. Trim batting and backing to ¼" beyond raw edge of quilt top. This will add fullness to binding.

2. Join binding strips to make one continuous strip if needed. To join, place strips perpendicular to each other, right sides together, and draw a diagonal line. Sew on drawn line and trim triangle extensions, leaving a ¼"-wide seam allowance. Continue stitching ends together to make the desired length. Press seams open.

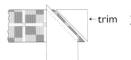
←trim

3. Fold and press binding strips in half lengthwise with wrong sides together.

4. Measure quilt through center from side to side. Cut two binding strips to this measurement. Lay binding strips on top and bottom edges of quilt top with raw edges of binding and quilt top aligned. Sew through all layers, ¼" from quilt edge. Press binding away from quilt top.

Front of Quilt

5. Measure quilt through center from top to bottom, including binding just added. Cut two binding strips to this measurement and sew to sides through all layers, including binding just added. Press.

6. Folding top and bottom first, fold binding around to back then repeat with sides. Press and pin in position. Hand-stitch binding in place using a blind stitch.

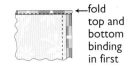
←fold top and bottom binding in first

Making Bias Strips

1. Refer to Fabric Requirements and Cutting Instructions for the amount of fabric required for the specific bias needed.

2. Remove selvages from the fabric piece and cut into a square. Mark edge with straight pin where selvages were removed as shown. Cut square once diagonally into two equal 45° triangles. (For larger squares, fold square in half diagonally and gently press fold. Open fabric square and cut on fold.)

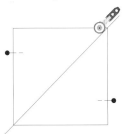

3. Place pinned edges right sides together and stitch along edge with a ¼" seam. Press seam open.

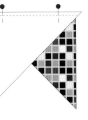

4. Using a ruler and rotary cutter, cut bias strips to width specified in quilt directions.

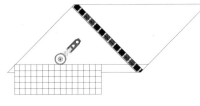

5. Each strip has a diagonal end. To join, place strips perpendicular to each other, right sides together, matching diagonal cut edges and allowing tips of angles to extend approximately ¼" beyond edges. Sew ¼"-wide seams. Continue stitching ends together to make the desired length. Press seams open. Cut strips into recommended lengths according to quilt directions.

Finishing Pillows

1. Layer batting between pillow top and lining. Baste. Hand or machine quilt as desired. Trim batting and lining even with raw edge of pillow top.

2. Narrow hem one long edge of each backing piece by folding under ¼" to wrong side. Press. Fold under ¼" again to wrong side. Press. Stitch along folded edge.

3. With sides up, lay one backing piece over second piece so hemmed edges overlap, making backing unit the same measurement as the pillow top. Baste backing pieces together at top and bottom where they overlap.

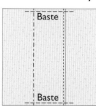

4. With right sides together, position and pin pillow top to backing. Using ¼"-wide seam, sew around edges, trim corners, turn right side out, and press.

Pillow Forms

Cut two pieces of fabric to size specified in project's materials needed list. Place right sides together, aligning raw edges. Using ¼"-wide seam, sew around all edges, leaving 5" opening for turning. Trim corners and turn right side out. Stuff to desired fullness with polyester fiberfill and hand-stitch opening closed.

Tips for Felting Wool

1. Wet wool fabric or WoolFelt™ with hot water. Do not mix colors as dyes may run.

2. Blot wool with a dry towel and place both towel and wool in dryer on high heat until thoroughly dry. The result is a thicker, fuller fabric that will give added texture to the wool. Pressing felted wool is not recommended, as it will flatten the texture. Most wools will shrink 15-30% when felted, adjust yardage accordingly.

Embroidery Stitch Guide

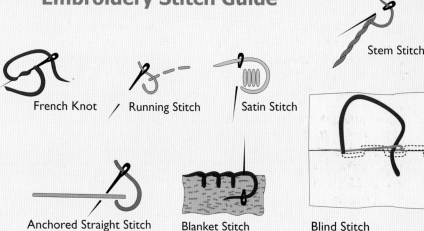

French Knot / Running Stitch / Satin Stitch / Stem Stitch / Anchored Straight Stitch / Blanket Stitch / Blind Stitch

Mistyfuse™

When fusing several layers of fusible web to a project, the quilt can become very stiff and hard to quilt. We used a new product for this quilt called 'Mistyfuse'. It is a very lightweight adhesive that doesn't add stiffness or weight to the quilt when adhered. It can be used on all types of fabrics - velvets to cotton, and delicates like tulles and organza. Follow manufacturer's instructions when using the product. Some additional items you will need are freezer paper and parchment paper or an appliqué pressing sheet. For more information go to www.mistyfuse.com.

General Painting Directions

Read all instructions on paint products before using and carefully follow manufacturer's instructions and warnings. For best results, allow paint to dry thoroughly between each coat and between processes unless directed otherwise. Wear face mask and safety goggles when sanding. Rubber gloves are recommended when handling stains and other finishing products.

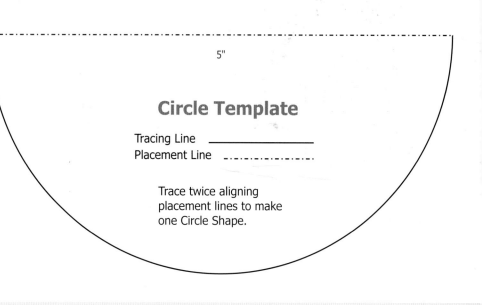

5"

Circle Template

Tracing Line _____

Placement Line _ . _ . _ . _ . _ . _ .

Trace twice aligning placement lines to make one Circle Shape.

About Debbie Mumm

A talented designer, author, and entrepreneur, Debbie Mumm has been creating charming artwork and quilt designs for more than twenty years.

Debbie got her start in the quilting industry in 1986 with her unique and simple-to-construct quilt patterns. Since that time, she has authored more than fifty books featuring quilting and home decorating projects and has led her business to become a multi-faceted enterprise that includes publishing, fabric design, and licensed art divisions.

Known world-wide for the many licensed products that feature her designs, Debbie loves to bring traditional elements together with fresh palettes and modern themes to create the look of today's country.

Designs by Debbie Mumm
Special thanks to my creative teams:

Editorial & Project Design
Carolyn Ogden: Publications & Marketing Manager
Nancy Kirkland: Quilt Designer/Seamstress
Georgie Gerl: Technical Writer/Editor
Anita Pederson: Machine Quilter

Book Design & Production
Monica Ziegler: Graphic Designer • Tom Harlow: Graphics Manager

Photography
Tom Harlow, Debbie Mumm® Graphics Studio
Carolyn Ogden: Photo Stylist

Art Team
Kathy Arbuckle: Artist/Designer • Gil-Jin Foster: Artist
Jackie Saling: Designer

Some furnishings provided by:
Gladys & Celia Hanning of Junebug Furniture and Design
junebugfurnitureanddesign.blogspot.com

The Debbie Mumm® Sewing Studio exclusively uses Bernina® sewing machines.

Library of Congress Control Number: 2010929146

Produced by:
Debbie Mumm, Inc.
1116 E. Westview Court
Spokane, WA 99218
(509) 466-3572
Fax (509) 466-6919

www.debbiemumm.com

Published by:
Leisure Arts, Inc
5701 Ranch Drive
Little Rock, AR • 72223
www.leisurearts.com

Discover More from Debbie Mumm®

Debbie Mumm's®
Quick Quilts for Home
112-page, soft cover

Debbie Mumm's®
I Care with Quilts
96-page, soft cover

Debbie Mumm's®
HomeComings
96-page, soft cover

Debbie Mumm's®
Cuddle Quilts for Little
Girls and Boys
96-page, soft cover

Available at local fabric and craft shops or at
debbiemumm.com